ENCOURAGING LANGUAGE DEVELOPMENT

CROOM HELM SPECIAL EDUCATION SERIES
Edited by Bill Gillham, Child Development Research Unit,
University of Nottingham

Already Available:

ENCOURAGING LANGUAGE DEVELOPMENT
Phyllis Hastings and Bessie Hayes

INDEPENDENCE TRAINING FOR VISUALLY HANDICAPPED
CHILDREN
Doris W. Tooze

Scheduled for Publication in Late 1981:

WORK PREPARATION FOR THE HANDICAPPED
David Hutchinson

TOYS AND PLAY FOR THE HANDICAPPED CHILD
Barbara Riddick

DAILY LIVING WITH THE HANDICAPPED CHILD
Diana Millard

TEACHING POOR READERS IN THE SECONDARY SCHOOL
Christine Cassell

Encouraging Language Development

PHYLLIS HASTINGS
AND
BESSIE HAYES

CROOM HELM LONDON

British Library Cataloguing in Publication Data

Hastings, Phyllis
    Encouraging·language development. — (Croom Helm
special education series).
    1. Children — Language
    I. Title   II. Hayes, Bessie
    401'.9   LB1139.L3

    ISBN   0-7099-0287-5

Printed in Great Britain by
Spottiswoode Ballantyne Ltd.,
Colchester and London

Contents

Series Foreword

The Croom Helm Special Education series is explicitly intended to give experienced practitioners in the helping services the opportunity to present a wide range of remedial programmes and techniques which they have developed in practice. The basis of the editorial policy is the belief that there exists much 'good practice' which is almost unknown beyond the local area where it is established. The present project is, therefore, concerned with the communication and dissemination of ideas and methods developed by those who use them in their working lives.

Encouraging Language Development focusses on parent-involvement in language remediation and the way in which this integrates with the conventional range of professional services.

B.G.

Preface

This book is written for all those professionals who are concerned to help parents whose children are slow in acquiring language; it is intended also to be of direct use to parents themselves.

There is great variation in the way children start to talk and sometimes parents worry unnecessarily, but on the whole they are among the first to be aware when there is a problem, in spite of well-meaning reassurances from doctors and friends.

When is there cause to worry? It is hard to lay down strict rules, but if a child is showing little sign of trying to use words by eighteen months, or short phrases by two and a half years, there *may* be a problem. If he has failed to make a reasonable start with talking by three years, then there is certainly cause for concern.

Sometimes slowness in talking goes along with or is caused by all sorts of other handicaps; sometimes it seems to be the only area in which the child has difficulty. Investigations may be necessary to sort out the child's problem, and he may need specialist help. Even if it is possible to arrange some professional help, however, the parent may feel that this is not enough. The speech therapist is unlikely to have enough time to do more than talk to parents occasionally about what they can do to help.

There is a very real sense in which, with a little guidance, the parents can be the most important experts of all. They are the ones in constant contact with the child, with a deep knowledge and understanding that no one else has of his moods, his expressions and his feelings. They know what 'makes him tick'. Language is a part of living and in the early stages only a little part of it can be taught artificially in lessons. Given some professional help, the parent is often the best person to build the foundations for language with his or her child.

We hope that this book will give both parents and professionals a broader understanding of how language develops, an understanding that will prove useful alongside any other help and guidance which may be available, and also when a parent is trying to help his or her child alone.

Throughout the book we speak of the child as 'he' and of the helping adult as 'the mother' or 'the parent(s)', but of course this is merely a useful shorthand. Any adult who is involved with the child, boy or girl, and who cares enough to try and help should be able to make use of the ideas we shall be talking about.

Acknowledgements

The main acknowledgement must be to those who helped us to produce the final manuscript: the series editor Bill Gillham; Margaret Grainger who typed the final draft; Nick Jessop who took most of the photographs and Sam Grainger who took those on pages 3, 17, 18 and 28, the parents and children, and the children and staff at the Cherryleas Assessment Centre, Leicester, who appear in the photographs; and those too numerous to mention who have commented helpfully on some or all of the manuscript at various stages in its progression.

P.H./B.H.

CHAPTER 1

What is Language?

Language is a part of being human. We are completely surrounded by it and the way we are able to use speech and language has an effect on how we are accepted by other people and on whether we can enjoy life to the full. *Talking* is the obvious part of language and it is when a child fails to talk as expected that everyone becomes concerned about him. Yet this is only the tip of the iceberg: there is far more to language than talking.

Words, on their own and in combination, enable people to communicate feelings, ideas and wishes and to influence one another. But a shared understanding of these things is building up gradually between a mother and her baby long before the baby can use any words. Parents read meaning into their baby's actions and responses from the moment of birth, and early on they can make a good guess as to whether the baby is understanding *them*. The richness of this 'communication before words' influences how well the words, when they come, will be used.

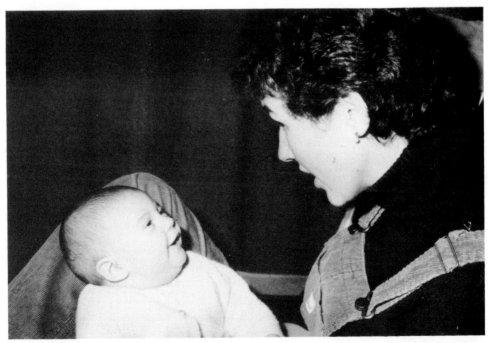

Very soon words themselves become important, because they enable the child to develop his thinking. They help him to notice people, objects, and events, to concentrate and remember, to sort out 'problems' and to see connections between things that happen. A limited amount of thinking can go on without words but many higher level ideas depend on words or other symbols. Language enters into almost all learning once the earliest stages of human development have passed, and the child with slow or defective speech and language may not be able to keep up with other children of his age.

As he grows, the child uses language in yet another way, internally, as if talking to himself. He compares new experiences with past happenings which he remembers, rehearses actions in his mind before doing them and decides which action to take according to what he thinks might happen. 'I can do this or that — but Mummy doesn't like me to do this — she will be cross — so I will do that.' Self control and 'being well-behaved' depend on this kind of internal language and it is little wonder that the child who is slow in talking often seems impulsive, erratic and confused.

Slowness in talking often brings with it other problems. A child may find it hard to get on with other children, especially in new settings, and may not be fully accepted by them, leading to frustration and unhappiness and often to difficult behaviour. Similarly, the child may have learned how to interpret gestures and signs and how to deal with familiar situations, but he may have much more difficulty than we realise in understanding what is *said* to him. Slight changes or new instructions may confuse him. He may find it hard to develop his thinking and to control and organise his behaviour.

Learning to be a Person

Let us go back to think about the time in a baby's life before he can talk, or understand words. How does he learn to get along with people?

In the first week or two of life many of the baby's actions would happen whether there was someone there or not. Sleeping and waking, sucking, crying, smiling, eye movements and periods of activity with kicking and arm-flailing, all come and go regularly. The baby has short periods of sucking and smiling, when he is both asleep and awake, whether he is hungry or full. To begin with they do not have any particular meaning. The relatives who claim, 'It's wind' are just as deceived as the mother who thinks that her new-born baby is smiling at her. Gradually the baby's actions do acquire meaning, and various activities, instead of being 'switched on and off', become linked to things which are happening to him. For example, he begins to smile — sometimes, but not always — when he hears a high-pitched voice, when something touches his leg, or when someone leans over him. From the early days he shows more interest in a human face than in many of the other things around him. Because of this, and because his mother values his smile and works to get him to respond to her, at around six to eight weeks the baby begins to smile regularly in response to a smiling face. His smile is now socially meaningful, and he goes on to become more discriminating in the way he uses it. And so, gradually, the baby is drawn into being responsive and into reacting to other human beings.

There is a similar pattern in early speech and language development. Even in the early months there is a noticeable difference between the baby's reactions to people and his reactions to objects. If a person is playing with him he makes movements of his lips and tongue, which he does not make to his toys, as if he is 'intending' to speak. A sensitive mother works to get her baby to respond to her, often without realising it, smiling and cooing at him and imitating many of his actions or sounds. She notices that his interest has been caught by something and comments on it. She talks to him gently shows him things. She plays simple games like 'Peek-a-boo' or 'I'm coming' as she moves towards him and touches him. All

the time she is sharing and conveying moods and activities, raising expectations, letting the baby know what she wants of him, leaving gaps in her talking and activity so that the baby can take part and do something. This pattern of, '*I* do something and then I wait for *you* to do something', is really a kind of conversation, both in sound and action, long before the baby can understand or use words. Gestures, moods, facial expressions, body contacts, tone of voice and shared interest all go towards building closeness and understanding between parent and child. Through this kind of contact the baby learns how to understand another person and then how to play and explore. He begins to acquire new experiences and the way is paved for speech and language to develop.

How Does Language Normally Develop?

As every mother knows there are great differences between individual children, and even children who are coming along well will vary a lot in the age at which they do things. Nevertheless, there is a general pattern in the way language normally develops and it will be helpful to look at this before thinking about what might have gone wrong for a particular child .

First Sounds

The baby's first sounds are cries and yawns, sneezes and hiccups, belches and gurgles. As he grows the variety increases and around three months he begins to play with sound-making, clicking his tongue, blowing bubbles, laughing and cooing. He is practising, through play, to control the fine movements of his tongue, lips and throat which at a later stage he will use in the making of speech sounds. By about eight weeks he is already being influenced by the sounds he hears. He gradually drops the sounds which do not appear in the particular language around him, though a baby of a different nationality might go on making them.

To begin with he depends a lot on *tone and loudness*. A harsh voice will cause him to flinch and cry, even though it may be saying something pleasant. Later on he learns to make his voice go up and down as if he is talking, before he is using words or making sense. It is as if he learns the tune of language before he learns the words. He will begin to use sounds, usually vowel sounds like 'ah' or 'uh', in a demanding way when he wants something, or in a calling way when he is trying to attract attention. Although he has no words, he understands that there is some meaning in the tone and in the rise and fall of the voices around him.

By five or six months the baby is taking enough interest in the sounds around him to turn towards them and he will gradually become more and more efficient at spotting exactly where a sound is coming from. Because he often finds that sounds are made by interesting things, like a toy or his mother's smiling face, he learns to listen and pay attention to sound.

First Words

Somewhere around nine to twelve months the baby begins using a sound which his mother interprets as meaning something and she repeats it and links it with an object or person. Perhaps it is 'daddy' or 'dog' or 'baby'. At first it may not sound much like the correct word but the mother knows he means something and repeats it with delight. She says the word correctly and the baby gradually improves his version. So the game of listening, copying and repeating sounds becomes more interesting.

The average child uses his first word at about twelve months, but there is *great* variation. Some perfectly normal children, about 8 per cent, say their first word by eight months while 5 per cent wait until after eighteen months. The first words are usually names of objects or people and for a while they remain few. Then the child slowly increases the number of words he uses and between about eighteen months and two years there is a rapid increase. By two years the average child will be using around two hundred words and will be able to understand several hundred more; but, again, the normal variation is considerable.

Words come singly at first, often linked with specific objects or people, used only when the object or person is in view. 'Teddy' for example means his particular one and it may be a month or two before the child will use it of another teddy. Gradually he begins to apply his words to similar things within a group and he will learn to call all cats 'cat'. He may then for a time include too many things and call all four-legged animals 'cat' or, embarrassingly, all men 'Daddy'. This is soon corrected as he increases his vocabulary and his knowledge of the world.

As he uses more words the child learns different kinds of words. Nouns and verbs come first and then prepositions, pronouns and adjectives, and so on.

Putting Words Together

The first word combinations are really used as a single unit — 'all gone', 'all fall down'. Then the child begins to put two words with separate meanings together. Often the first word of the pair is a well-used one which he starts to apply to a range of things — 'Daddy gone', 'Daddy car', 'Daddy up' or 'more dinner', 'more biccy', 'more please'. He may use the same two words to mean different things. For example, 'Daddy-coat' may mean 'There is Daddy's coat' or 'Help me put my coat on, Daddy', according to where and how he says it. And the same event may provoke different comments: his father going to work, for example, may result in 'Daddy car', 'Daddy gone' or 'Daddy work'.

Children vary a great deal in the way they develop and use their first words but by the age of two years most children are able to put two words together with meaning.

From an early age the child will have enjoyed listening to rhymes and jingles with lots of repetition and rhythm. Now he begins to take part, doing the actions and adding the final words of each section. He likes the same stories repeated with no detail changed.

From two to three years the child's sentences begin to grow. He says things like 'boy kick ball' or 'give ball Mummy'. The 'linking' words of speech such as 'the',

'to' and 'is' begin to appear. Throughout this time the child is steadily learning to understand more and he can follow longer sentences in the conversation of those around him. Most parents are familiar with the stage where the child seems to be asking questions constantly. 'What?' questions usually start around two years, 'Where?' and 'Who?' questions around three years and 'Why?' questions around four. Often the child goes on with his questions even when he has been answered. He already knows the answer and seems to want to hear the reply over and over again, perhaps in a different way.

Pronunciation

During the early years the child makes many 'incorrect' sounds as he acquires words. Some children are much more unclear than others, but this is just a normal feature of immaturity and as adults repeat what the child says, but more clearly, so he will gradually adapt his version to sound more like theirs. He may not become completely clear until he is five- or six-years-old. Many children starting school are still making mistakes with some of the more difficult sounds.

The ability to make sounds develops in a certain order. Usually the sounds made at the front of the mouth are produced first, then the middle sounds and then the back sounds. Combinations of sounds, such as *sm*, *str*, *cl*, *ch*, and *th* always develop later and may not be used correctly until well after the child has started school. Often, if a child finds a particular sound difficult he substitutes one that is easier and that he can manage well, so we get words like 'fin' for 'thin' or 'lellow' for 'yellow'. This kind of unclearness will sort itself out as he grows and the correctness of pronunciation will go on improving long after the child is fluent in using language.

Some children go through a short phase of stammering when they repeat the first syllable or part of a word many times, and they often talk in a disjointed, hesitant or very rapid fashion. This stage is difficult for parents to ignore but in the great majority of cases it will quickly disappear if not too much is made of it.

Helping Language to Grow

From two to five years the child's language continues to develop, both on the understanding side and in the use of longer sentences, so that by the time he reaches school age the average child can construct five or six word sentences and use them to explain quite complicated ideas. The achievement is a truly remarkable one. Of course, the child brings a great deal to the experience of language — to some extent it is 'in' him to acquire language. But it is clear that this gradual process of learning to speak is influenced by what the child is hearing around him and by what he is learning about the world. If his questions are answered with simple, clear explanations and if he is helped to reason out ideas and to explore and discover things beyond the limited home environment, then his vocabulary will be wider and his ability to express himself and describe his experiences will be encouraged.

When Language Fails to Develop

An appreciation of normal language development provides the basic framework for considering problems children may have in acquiring language. We can only know that a problem exists if we have some idea of what is more or less 'normal'. Many things can interfere with a child's ability to acquire language in the usual way. A particular child may show one of the following problems, or a mixture of them. The first step should be to get help in sorting things out as far as possible (see Chapter 4).

Hearing Losses

A child may have a severe or a partial hearing loss. A deaf baby typically behaves much like a hearing baby in his sound-making and playing with sound until he is about six-months-old. After that the range of sounds he makes decreases, and his eyes become very active. If the hearing loss is a moderate one the baby hears some of what goes on around him but in a distorted way, which is difficult to make sense of. Or he may have a variable loss, worse when he has colds and infections, but clearing up in between.

Any hearing loss, particularly during the first two or three years, can play havoc with the process of acquiring language. Not only does it prevent the child hearing sounds, but it also means that he cannot listen to *himself* and improve his own attempts at words. Clearly, if there are any doubts, the first step must be a careful examination. If the problem turns out to be severe then the child may need very specialised teaching and help. If it is less severe then many of the suggestions in this book may prove helpful, keeping in mind the child's particular difficulties.

Brain Damage and Other Physical Causes

There are a few conditions, such as a cleft palate or a malformation of the jaw, which interfere directly with the ability to speak. These may need surgical correction and will also need the help of a speech therapist. Tongue-tie is very rarely a cause of speech impairment, so much so that, unless the child also has great problems with eating, it should be dismissed as a possible cause.

A good many children who suffer from varying degrees of cerebral palsy, which affects movement, also have difficulties with speech and language. Problems may also occur when there has been damage to other parts of the brain or its associated nerves, but where there may be no obvious physical results. Such damage usually occurs before, during or shortly after birth, but in an individual case it will probably be impossible to be sure precisely what has gone wrong. All we may know is that the child has difficulty in understanding, remembering or producing speech. We can usually only guess at such a cause and it is not possible to put such things right. Instead we have to concentrate on helping the child with his language as much as possible.

Mental Retardation

A child may be generally retarded and slow-learning. His mental growth is slower than his physical growth and because of this he will probably be slower in talking. Without language a child may appear even duller and more backward than he is, and unless we try to help him to develop language as far as he is able he may actually *become* duller because his thinking is not developing. Such children can be helped, and with carefully structured teaching* they usually show slow but steady improvement.

*See Bill Gillham (1979) *The First Words Language Programme* (London: George Allen & Unwin).

Emotional and Relationship Difficulties

Some children have problems affecting not only their speech but also their behaviour and way of relating to people. A child may be excessively withdrawn or timid, avoiding contact with other people. In an extreme form he may seem cut off from contact, absorbed in repetitive activities and mannerisms. Such children may talk in some circumstances but not in others. With children like these some of the suggestions in this book may be helpful, but you will also need to seek advice from a psychologist, psychiatrist or social worker.

Possible Signs of Trouble in the Baby's Early Days

Some slow talkers have a history of being 'too good' as babies, content to lie quietly in the pram, failing to get the stimulation from contact with other people which is needed for healthy development. Others are restless, over-active and 'difficult' babies from the start, quite exhausting to those around them. In either case this influences the way that mother and baby get on together, without it being anyone's fault.

Many of these children have early feeding difficulties, sometimes because the muscles and 'machinery' for eating are not quite working properly. Sucking, chewing and swallowing may not be easy for them and unpleasant feelings may come to be associated with mouth, nose and throat. Such children are often reluctant to experiment with sound and make fewer babbling and gurgling noises than the average baby. Some children do not play naturally and need to be taught a great many of the things normally taken for granted. Many do not attend well either in listening or looking and consequently take less interest in their environment and learn less from it.

What is the Problem?

Even after extensive and careful investigations it is not always possible to explain *why* a child's difficulties have arisen. But explanations are not always important: it is much more useful to look closely at what the problem is *now*, and to think what we might do to improve things. On the whole, speech and language problems fall into two main types.

(1) Delayed Language. Here comprehension (understanding) or expression (speaking) or both, are delayed and are below the level we would expect from the child's general ability. The child is following a normal pattern in acquiring language but he is well behind where he should be at his age. He may have periods when he seems stuck and is making no progress.

(2) Deviant Language. Here, in addition to delay, the child is showing uneven and disordered language development. For example, he may have difficulty in combining sounds or words in the normal order or in joining sounds together to make words. He may have great difficulty in understanding what he hears, or in saying words even though he understands them. There are gaps in his language development and he is not following the usual pattern.

Accepting the Situation

The realisation that some part of their child's development is not normal produces in parents a welter of feelings and is often surrounded by other pressures and fears. Relatives or friends may try to reassure them that there really is no problem, when they know that there is, or may suggest things to worry about that had not occurred to them. The parents' main concern may be about schooling, even though that is years ahead. They may feel that there is some family problem that has been passed on to the child and feel guilty in consequence. Sometimes parents do worry quite unnecessarily; because of lack of experience of other children they may expect too much of their child when he is really progressing normally. More often, however, parents *do* know when there is a problem.

Parents can help their child most by accepting that the problem is real; it is there to be tackled and understood rather than explained away. Acceptance is not easy. We all want our children to be 'normal' and it is natural to keep hoping that in a few months or years things will come right without our having to do anything about it. There may be other children in the family, and little time to think about or work on this child's problems; parents may feel they could not cope with anything extra. The child may be difficult or upsetting, or irritating, or else so pathetic that they spoil him and try to pretend that the problem does not matter. The situation is further complicated by the fact that many parents blame themselves when a child is slow in talking, and unfortunately relatives and friends, and even some professionals from whom they seek help, may do the same.

There are very few cases where there is any real blame to be attached. If a mother had shut her child away in a darkened room and allowed him little or no contact with the world around him, then she would be to blame for his poor development. But it is rarely anything like that. More often the feelings of blame are because the mother wonders whether she ought to have noticed much earlier that things were not right. She may feel that she ought not to have allowed others in the family to cover up the child's needs by talking for him, understanding him too easily. She may worry about the effects of leaving him with a baby-minder, of giving him less attention when another baby arrived, of not providing him with enough stimulating toys and experiences, or simply of not spending enough time with him for various reasons. These are real and worrying feelings, shared by many mothers. However, blaming people is rarely useful and is often hurtful and unfair. It is easier to accept that things are not all the parent's fault when we realise that the child who is learning to talk normally gets his mother to teach him by the way he behaves. The child with a language problem cannot or does not prompt and influence his parents in that way so that they are left wondering where to begin.

We take for granted the fascinating process that usually goes on quite unconsciously between mother and child. It is a two-way process and the mother knows the level of speech she must use because the child is demanding it from her. If one side of this process is not functioning well then the whole interaction goes wrong. If the child is slow in making sounds then often the mother becomes less talkative too; it is very difficult (because unrewarding) to keep up a one-sided conversation.

Another factor is that normally the stage of babbling and action games comes at a time when the baby is frequently picked up, carried around or bounced on his mother's knee. By the time the child with delayed speech is ready for this stage he is already quite large, used to running about and reluctant to be held still for any length of time. His mother is also treating him instinctively like an older child and is reluctant to go back to the simple speech games that he is now ready for. It is therefore much more difficult to build up the two-way process.

The child with a language problem may not ask questions, or he may be very late in doing so. He may be a relatively silent child and it is then very difficult for his parents to know what to talk about that will interest him. If his vocabulary is limited to a few words then, because adults around are trying to respond to the child, these few words may become the centre of all conversation, limiting the subjects and ideas that the child is hearing about.

It is important to realise, in helping the slow talker, that somehow a different approach has to be tried. Parents have to work out what the child is ready for, and go back to earlier stages of development with him when he needs it. It is no good trying to build language without first making sure that the foundations are sound. This may mean that initially little in the way of sounds or words is expected from the child, that all the work is being done at an earlier stage which may involve teaching him to listen or to imitate, or to find meaning in toys and simple play. Or, at a more advanced stage, it may mean thinking of ways of teaching the child to use longer sentences before demanding that every sound is made correctly. Objectives have to be appropriate to the stage of development. Helping the child in more indirect ways may be far more effective than 'teaching him to talk'.

Properly organised, encouraging language development need not be a time-consuming process. Very often it is not *more* time with the child that is needed but a rather different use of the time the parents would normally spend, or a rearrangement of the things they fit in to the day. Usually teaching is most effective within the routine activities and ordinary everyday situations of the home. Whatever the parents plan to do to help their child must fit into their daily life without strain, so the plans must be small-scale and feasible. This may mean a few minutes extra time spent with the child at bedtime, or the limiting of television time so that a little game can be played. Encouraging the child to listen and look and talk on trips to the shops, at bath times and meal times, is something that can be coped with even in a busy household, without the other members of the family suffering.

The Need for Parental Involvement

The reactions of parents to the knowledge that their child's language is not developing normally are as varied as the individual parents themselves. Some are sensible, competent and eager to help. Many would prefer to leave the problem in the hands of 'experts'. Some protest that the child will not do what they tell him and will take more notice of outsiders, so it is better if they are not involved. Others want to help but are over-anxious and try to push the child too hard.

Why is it so important that parents should be involved? There is a close bond between a child and his mother and father and it is within this relationship that language usually starts and grows. No therapy or teaching can replace or simulate the interaction that goes on between a child and his parents. A child learns to talk to satisfy his daily needs or for love and attention. He talks in order to control his family, to contribute, to take his part, to hold his own. In all his early experiences his mother and father are the main figures and the natural teachers. Parents normally spend more time with their child than anyone else does. Even if the child goes to nursery or playgroup, he is at home for many more hours than he is away from it. If his parents are not directly involved in encouraging his language development, a great deal of valuable time is being lost and the child may not be putting into practice what he is learning where it most matters — in living.

Relatives and friends often have a large part to play in the life of a family. Their concern may lead them to make comments or give advice, based maybe on old wives' tales or the reported experiences of others. If the parents are involved in helping and guiding their child, and come to understand something of what is going on, not only can they resist unwanted advice, but they can also encourage relatives to think along the same lines, so extending the situations where the child can be helped.

It is important that the child, who is often aware of his failures, should be given the chance to find out that he can be a success. Someone at home has to make him feel that his attempts to talk are appreciated and that he is making progress. It is so easy, through anxiety to help the child, to end up correcting everything he tries to say. If food or toys are withheld until he 'says it properly', or if he is pestered into talking and imitating, he ends up feeling cross and defeated. In some homes a busy mother may disregard a poor talker's speech attempts because it is hard to make out what he is saying, and so the child learns that a shout or a temper tantrum produces quicker results. Sometimes parents anticipate all their child's needs and make excuses for him. He, in turn, aware that they are unsure of his capabilities, feels insecure and uncertain about attempting to use them. The child's acquisition of language may be a slow process and he must gain pleasure and satisfaction at every step, so that he wants to keep on trying. He must be given confidence all along the way. Other children may tease him and it is at home that he needs to feel he can succeed. The parents need to be positive in accepting his attempts, not expecting perfection, but greeting any attempt at improvement with a show of pleasure.

Behaviour Difficulties

Finally, we must recognise that many language-handicapped children are indeed difficult and irritating and show behaviour which worries and upsets their parents. Often it is clear that the child's frustration at his inability to communicate lies at the root of the problem, but this understanding does not make it any easier. When parents are distressed, bewildered and uncertain about how to handle the child there is sometimes disagreement between them and inconsistency, which adds to his confusion and insecurity. Often the child develops a very negative view of himself as a 'naughty boy'.

There seem to be two main types of troublesome behaviour which may accompany language problems. The child may lean towards being withdrawn and solitary or he may be aggressive and obstinate. Some children alternate from one extreme to the other, and others show quite different behaviour in different situations. Sometimes the child becomes abnormally dependent and clinging, behaving in a babyish way and making a great fuss about being left. He reacts to frustration, or any disturbance of his routines, with tantrums and tears. He may show an embarrassing kind of shyness which is 'put on' rather than genuine. As he grows he tends to be lonely and socially isolated, even when he has the opportunity to mix with other children, because of the difficulties he has in relating and communicating. Daydreaming and vagueness are common, as are minor mannerisms and rituals.

At the other extreme the outgoing child bangs and shouts and hits out. He seems to refuse to conform on principle and can become a most unlikeable child. He is fighting the world, but much of his bad behaviour is because he does not know what is expected of him or cannot take part effectively. His actions are easily misinterpreted. The child who cannot go up to others and join in a conversation may well touch or push or shout in a disruptive way, when all he is trying to do is to make contact or persuade. He gets used to rebuffs and takes an aggressive stance in anticipation of them. Such a child is likely to be restless and over-active

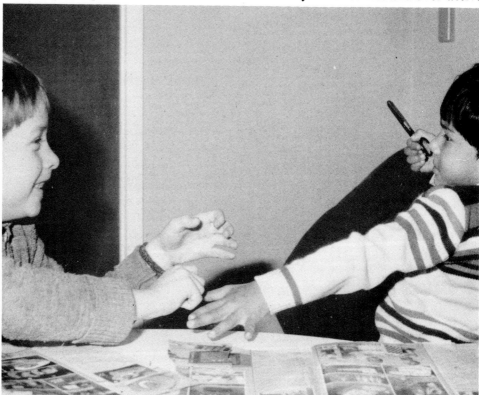

because he cannot concentrate. He cannot settle to play and flits around from one thing to another, interrupting other children's activities. Without language many of the activities suitable for his age level are unrewarding for him. Sometimes, although the bad behaviour undoubtedly arose as a by-product of the communication difficulty, it has long since become an end in itself. Tempers are rewarding because they release anger and get attention and they may have proved successful in getting the child what he wanted in the past.

Of course these behaviours also occur in children who can talk perfectly well, and there are some children with delayed speech whose behaviour gives no cause for concern. Nevertheless, these patterns are common with speech and language disorders. If they are severe it may be advisable for the parents to seek help with the management of a child's behaviour at the same time as he is being helped to communicate better. Fortunately, we nearly always find that as language develops the child's behaviour also improves.

CHAPTER 2

Back to Basics

With a child whose speech is delayed it is usually necessary to go back to the simple early stages, to put in some of the missing foundations for language, and it is often important to keep on with simple activities for a much longer time than with other children. The basic processes have to be well established *before* more direct speech and language teaching can be effective. If you are reading this with a particular child in mind, you may feel that he has successfully developed beyond the stage we shall be talking about in the present chapter, but think it through carefully and do not take this for granted. There may be gaps, and the child may need help or practice in some areas and yet be doing quite well in others.

When parents are worried that their child is slow to talk they often work very hard to teach him to copy words. But this may be taking things in the wrong order. Continually demanding that the child 'say' things will often 'freeze' his development, and he will resist being taught in this way. So, what should we be doing to encourage him to talk?

We want the child to enjoy making sound, and ways are suggested to encourage this, but at the same time it is important to take the emphasis off what is *coming out* of the child and to place it on what is *going in*. Talking is not the starting point in the process and a good understanding of language must come first. The child must be able to look and to listen, to relate to people and respond, and then the most important thing to teach is the *understanding* of language; the ability to make sense of things.

Many things contribute to a child's growing understanding of the world around him and his own experiences. It is convenient to look at some of them under different headings but there is a great deal of overlap in the following sections, and ideas used to encourage one thing may also help in other areas. For ease of style the suggestions that follow are written as if addressed directly to the adult engaging in the activities.

Learning to Get on with People

Getting along with people starts long before a child can carry on a conversation in words. If parents can give their child plenty of practice in situations where, 'I do something and then you do something', or, 'You do something and it makes me do something', then they will be laying useful foundations on which conversations can be built later, when the words come.

One of the earliest games which babies enjoy is that of giving things and taking them back. You can start a child off with a group of objects, such as blocks or spoons or buttons, and holding your hand out say, 'Give me one please', with appropriate gestures to show what is meant. If to begin with he does not get the

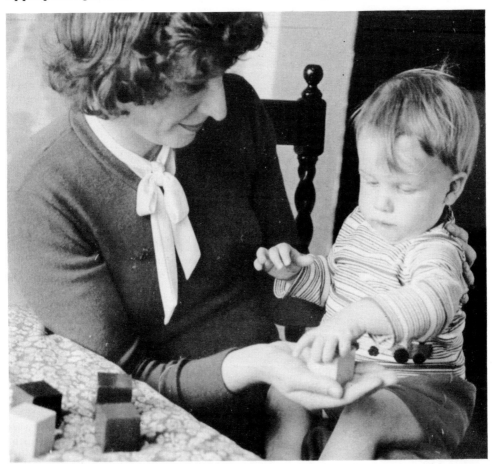

idea, take his hand gently and do the actions for him. Then show pleasure and say, 'Thank you'. Repeat this several times, and then give the objects back to him one by one. Try to encourage him to make a sound with you for 'please' and 'thank you' each time — any sound at all will do to begin with. Later on the game can be extended by putting objects into a box or basket and taking them out one at a time. Try to get the child to roll a big ball back to you when you roll it to him. Again, you may have to do the actions for him the first few times but he will soon get the idea. Then move on to throwing and catching, talking about what you are doing in simple short sentences.

Children love games such as 'Peek-a-boo' or 'Round and round the garden' and once they become familiar you can increase the enjoyment by drawing out

the suspense — 'Oh, dear. Where has she gone?' — then a long pause before the final 'Peek-a-boo'. Familiar nursery rhymes can be used in the same way. 'Ring a ring a roses, all fall . . .' and a long pause before the 'down'. Hold the child's hands and sit on the floor with him, pulling backwards and forwards as you sing 'See-saw Margery Daw', letting him take over more of the action as soon as you feel he is taking part.

Repetition plays a big part in children's early learning, and nursery rhymes and stories which have frequently repeated phrases become much loved. Parents may get tired of them but the child will not. Once the child recognises the rhymes he can be encouraged to take part, with the adult saying most of the rhyme but leaving a gap for the last word of each line. If the child makes any kind of sound at the appropriate time, he is joining in. It doesn't matter if to begin with it does not sound like the right word. When the rhymes have actions, all the better. You can get the child to put in the actions, with an attempt at the words at the same time.

Physical Contact

Physical contact is an important part of early games. Talking, when it comes, is a way of reaching out and making contact with people. Before speech, the same kind of reaching out and sharing ideas and activities can go on in the form of touching, watching and following what others are doing.

There are many simple games where parents can be in close contact with their child, but it should not be *too* close. If you hug him to you all the time he cannot learn how to react to you. Many games can be played with the child sitting on your knee, or on a chair, facing you. While you play you are teaching him to listen, to watch your face and to respond to what you do. Jog him gently on your knee: 'A farmer's horse goes trot, trot, trot'. Gradually increase to a gallop, talking as you go, stopping and starting, making him anticipate, so that he waits eagerly for your next move. Hand-clapping games such as 'Pat-a-cake' or 'This little piggy went to market' all encourage looking and listening, expecting and waiting.

Play around on the floor with bigger actions. Play chasing games or give the child a ride on your back, altering your pace from time to time describing where you are going or getting the child to direct you in any way he can. Do not let such games get too noisy and exciting or the child will not be listening, watching and responding. Instead he may get over-excited and the game may end in tears.

Dressing and undressing time is a great opportunity for body contact, while learning to co-operate and to practise such language skills as attending, anticipating and remembering. In a busy household these can be hectic times, to be got through as quickly as possible, but time can be made for various enjoyable activities, once their importance is understood.

'Peek-a-boo' can be played as clothes are pulled over the head. Arms disappear into sleeves and can be watched for coming out. This can be great fun if you pretend they are trains going through tunnels and talk about them and make

appropriate noises. Socks can be pulled off quickly or slowly while talking about what you are doing and watching for the wriggling toes to appear.

Encouraging Attention

Most children with language difficulties fail to make the best possible use of what they can see and hear because they are not noticing or attending properly. They flit about from one thing to another, or they are easily distracted from whatever they are doing by other things going on around them. They need to learn how to listen and to look, to recognise many different sights and sounds, and to shut out and ignore all the other confusing things around them while concentrating on one thing.

To begin with, when you want the child to concentrate on a particular toy, clear the space around of other toys or distractions. In your activities only expect short periods of concentration, with quick success for the child. Do not talk too much or you will distract him. As he improves you can begin to talk more about what he is doing, commenting or giving him instructions. Increase the demands for attention and concentration only gradually, being ready to go back to simpler games and activities for a while when he becomes distractible.

From the earliest days it is helpful if the child can have some toys which make sounds. There are rattles and musical boxes, but containers filled with a variety of things — pebbles, peas, rice, flour and so on — are just as good as more expensive toys. His interest can be caught by getting him to notice the different sounds when he taps or shakes things, bangs them on different surfaces or drops them.

Then the child can be encouraged to notice the sounds around him when his mother points them out, comments on them and listens herself. At home there are the sounds of the clock, the door or telephone bell, the kettle boiling, the tap running, a spoon on a plate at dinner time, someone going upstairs and countless more. On walks there are bird noises, dogs barking, bicycle bells, car noises, fluttering leaves and clicking gates. Games of 'What was that sound?' or 'Where is it?' can be played. Get the child to look around and find where the aeroplane is, the ice-cream van, the sweet being unwrapped out of sight. He may enjoy games like listening for you to tap on the other side of a door so that he can tell you to come in.

Watching is important too. He will like hand puppets or teddy bears which hide and pop out from unpredictable places behind a chair covered by a towel, demanding a clap or 'Hello' when seen. It is fun to draw tiny details such as a ladybird or a spider in unlikely places, somewhere on each page of a favourite book. Then you can look at the book together, searching for the insects. Play at blowing soap bubbles, getting the child to watch a particular bubble carefully all the way down, saying 'Pop' as it touches the ground and bursts. You can tape-record the sounds of various toys and then get the child to point out the toy as he hears the sound.

Many children are inattentive because they are impulsive and cannot wait. They grab at things, or try to do puzzles in a haphazard way, without letting their eyes guide their hands. Or they take in the first few words of what is said to them and never listen to the complete message. Games which encourage looking at or listening to all the alternatives before choosing one can be useful here. A gentle restraining hand on the child's hands until he has looked at all the materials in front of him and listened to the end of the instructions will help.

Some games have a built-in delay, as when the child has to watch for a particular sign or listen for a particular sound before doing something. 'When I make this sound _____ then you can go for the sweet.' As the child gets better at such games the signal can be made fainter and longer-delayed, requiring closer listening or looking, and the description of where the sweet is to be found can be made more complicated.

A child needs as many cues as possible in order to understand what you are saying. Watching lip movements and facial expressions can round out what he is hearing, and if he looks at you when you are talking to him he is more likely to keep listening until you have finished. Making sure that he is watching, you can start with early games on your knee. Later on he may need reminding to keep looking at you. Stop and wait if he looks away and try to keep his attention to the end of what you are saying. You may need to turn his face gently towards you to remind him. In play with music try to get him to respond to differences in speed,

rhythm and loudness. Movement and dancing, with big, noisy movements and quiet, tiny ones, quick steps, slow steps, clapping hands in time to the rhythms — all this will make him listen more carefully in a pleasant, enjoyable way.

As the child becomes more aware of sounds you can play more difficult games, where you ring a bell, clap your hands or make other sounds in various parts of the room, while he keeps his eyes closed. You move back to his side, he opens his eyes and has to point to or say where the sound came from. Let him test you out in the same way when he is able. Or you can hide things which make sounds such as an alarm clock, a kitchen timer or a wind-up toy and get him to find them. At first make it easy. Hide the clock under a box or a cloth in front of him and ask, 'Where is it?' Then go on to make it more difficult, hiding it under one of two or three boxes so that he has to listen hard to find the right one. Then it can be behind chairs or in cupboards, making it a real searching game with careful listening and localising.

Talking to the Child

Early on the child is very dependent on his parents teaching him by talking *to* him. The general flow of conversation around him is likely to be too fast and too complicated for him to get much from it. There are lots of ways in which you can help him to make sense of it gradually, by the way you talk to him. Try to keep talking to him even if to begin with you are getting little from him in return. Talk clearly and not too quickly in simple, short sentences, about things which are actually there in front of him or are happening at the time. Put the emphasis on the important words and do not be afraid to repeat things, possibly with slight variations in the way you say them. On the other hand avoid chattering away at him so constantly that he could not get a word in edgeways even if he wanted to! Leave some gaps when you look at him and act if you expect an answer. Respond in a pleased way to any sounds he makes in his attempts to communicate with you. In talking use plenty of expression, letting your voice rise and fall, so that your child will be interested even before he understands the words. Try to think how simple 'teaching language' can be used in everyday living. For example, let us look at two bits of conversation which might be used prior to going out shopping.

The first mother says, 'Come on, hurry up, because I want to get down to the shops early today so that we can be back in time for dinner. Now don't be silly. Go and get your coat at once or we'll be late.' The second mother says, 'Come on Johnny. Get ready. We're going out. Time for the shops. Coat on. Find your coat. Help me to put it on. Open the door. Hurry. We're going shopping.'

In the first example the mother is using a great many words, spoken rapidly. In the second she has cut her language down into short phrases with a pause between each and she is talking about what they are doing. The second way is much more effective for a child having difficulty with language. This way of reducing language is easily learned and enables a mother to teach her child in a great many everyday situations.

It is often a good idea to repeat a phrase you have used or to alter it only slightly as if you are talking to youself, slowly and extra clearly. 'Orange juice. Here's your orange juice. Drink your orange juice up.' Talk in a similar way about anything the child shows an interest in. For example, a great deal of language can be taught in playing with toys cars. 'Drive the car' (actions with appropriate *brrm brrm* noises). 'Peep, peep, goes the horn. Push the car. Round the corner. Stop. All get out. Shut the door. Bang. Drive it away.'

Use the same phrases regularly with everyday activities. At bath time, 'Wash your hands. Wash your face. Round and round. Now your feet. Out you jump. Rub your legs with the towel.'

Build up a collection of words and phrases, which are frequently used in familiar situations. For example, 'All gone. Oh, dear. Hello Daddy. Bye bye. All fall down. Go away doggie. More, please. Again. Thank you. Another one. Drink, please. Biscuit, please.' As phrases become firmly associated with situations the child will expect them and they will become meaningful.

Use gestures *as you talk*, giving the child clues that he can see and which he can associate with words as a help to interpreting their meaning. Some parents are afraid of using signs, but as long as you are using the gestures *alongside* words, to help out with meaning and not *instead of* words, they are helpful, not harmful.

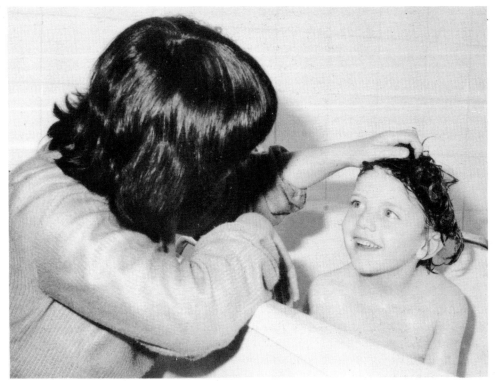

You can, for example, rock your arms as you talk about a baby, hold an imaginary telephone receiver to your ear when talking about the telephone or put your hands to one ear and close your eyes when talking about going to sleep.

Try to get into the habit of doing BBC-type running commentaries, simplifying your language in the way we have talked about, as you do the washing up or make a cup of tea. Talk to the child about what you are doing as you go shopping or walk to the park. Make a scrapbook of familiar activities with pictures cut from catalogues or magazines, so that you can sit and look at it together and you can talk about activities you know are meaningful for him. Draw things for the child, talking about them as you go. It will not matter to him if you are not much of an artist. 'Look, let's put a hat on the man. Here is his little dog. This is his house. It needs some windows. What else?'

Try to get the child to follow simple instructions by asking him to bring things for you, at first by pointing to them as you say the words, later by giving him increasingly difficult directions about how to find the thing you want, without using gestures. A toy telephone can be a great help in getting some reluctant children to take part in games and to attempt conversations, as can simple glove puppets, made of old socks with eyes stitched on.

Language helps to develop a child's ability to think and teaches him connections between events, people and places. In order to develop his mental skills you can be constantly making use of situations about the house and regular 'out and about' situations. So often our instructions to a child throughout the day tend to

be negative and corrective. 'Don't do that. Stop it. Be quiet.' A positive instruction always works better if you can remember to put it that way, and is less likely to antagonise the child. Remember to say 'Walk on the pavement' rather than 'Don't walk in the road'. Further than this, try to make your talking to the child contain more than instructions. So much can be taught by quietly talking about the interesting sights and sounds and happenings in the park or the garden, the street or the shop.

Encouraging Vocalisation

Encouraging a child to make sounds must essentially be a happy process or it will not work. The babbling of a small baby happens when he is relaxed and contented, when he is happily excited or when some object or person who gives pleasure comes into his line of vision. When feeling strange or self-conscious the baby is usually silent, often defiantly so. Where there has been delay in the production of sounds, attempts to make sounds should be encouraged in an easy-going, natural setting.

There are a number of different possible causes for a child's failure to produce sounds. If a child is *very* silent most of the time and seems to be using only one or two different sounds when he does try, then the parents should seek professional help before going too far in trying to encourage him themselves.

There is some basic muscular training the parents can help with, which at first may seem to have little to do with talking. It is however very important and the connection soon becomes apparent. Watch, carefully but unobtrusively, the way the child eats. He should be developing good grown-up ways of chewing and swallowing. He must gradually leave behind the baby ways of sucking with his tongue forward in his mouth, and the habit of trying to soften food by sucking at it rather than chewing it. It is important therefore to give him gradually harder foods, in larger pieces, so that he has to learn to chew. This will exercise the muscles of his jaw.

It is also wise not to allow the child to go on using a bottle or a feeder beaker for too long. It may be easier for the mother but it may get in the way of his develop-ing mature, controlled movements of his lips and tongue and throat — the very movements he will need in speaking. If the child is not yet drinking from a cup it is worthwhile spending more time in helping him to learn how to shape his lips round the edge of the cup and hold the liquid in his mouth by moving his lips. Help the child to feed correctly from a spoon, so that he is not just tipping sloppy food off the spoon into his mouth, but is actively drawing it into his mouth with his lips and cleaning the spoon. Then he has to remember to keep his lips closed while he chews. Many children chew with their mouth drooping open, and they may need a gentle reminder to pull their lips round to meet while they eat. Some-times this can be done by the mother actually helping the child to close his lips by touching them and just pushing them together. When the child is praised for co-operating he is usually quite happy with this activity. The muscles of the lips, the tongue and the jaw are in this way being trained to move correctly, and they are then in the right condition to be used to make the complicated movements necessary for speech.

We know that meal times can be tiring and difficult, without any added activities to teach, so approach this slowly. If you begin by watching how the child eats and drinks you can see if you can improve one small area at a time. If however, you find that it is making you anxious and meal times are a struggle anyway, leave well alone or you may do more harm than good. Concentrate on introducing more demanding and varied foods into your child's diet and perhaps ask for some advice from the Speech Therapy or School Psychological Service.

The child can be encouraged to make more use of his lips, tongue, teeth, facial muscles and other parts used in speaking by all sorts of games. Blowing bubbles, sucking up and holding bits of paper with a straw, putting screwed-up paper in the end of a straw and blowing it out. 'Simon says'-type copying games using 'raspberries', car noises and other lip-produced sounds, or with pulled faces to be copied, are very useful. Another interestng activity is trying to lick spots of jam from various points around the lips. Get the child to stick his tongue out to lick a lollipop which you hold for him. The aim in all this is to get the child to make more use of the organs of speech and also to give him practice so that the move-ments gradually come under good control.

Mothers usually enjoy saying or singing nursery rhymes to their children, or singing popular songs as they work around the house. Singing-games are a very good way of teaching the child, not only in a casual way but quite deliberately when he is sitting on your knee or next to you on the settee, or when you are holding hands and jumping about. Expect him to join in with the rhyme or song and show your delight at any sounds he may use, even if they are very limited and repetitive. It is important for the child to be able to use his voice and produce something, even though to begin with it may only be a vowel sound, made very gruffly.

Watch for activities or situations that cause him to produce sounds and make use of them. It may be that for one child bath time is a good time to prolong and concentrate on, while for another it may be the half hour after his father comes home from work and some time set aside for play and attention then would pay dividends. The child needs to feel that his efforts to communicate by sound are worthwhile. Reward him by showing your pleasure and approval immediately. It does no harm to exaggerate your delight a little, but do not dwell on a particular sound production too much or you may inhibit him.

When a child begins to talk he uses a rather limited number of consonants and vowel sounds to begin with. This is completely normal and most children use certain sounds long before they are able to make others. For example, m,p,b,t,d,k and g come first, and usually as the first sound in a syllable, such as 'ba' or 'ma'. First word attempts are often babbled — 'bababa' or 'paba'. Continuous vocalisation can be encouraged by playing with babbling sounds, much as you would with a small baby, trying to get the child to play at making noises.

Gradually meaning can be put into the babble, for example by associating 'dadada' with Daddy. It is a good idea to work at introducing words which contain the child's babbled sounds. Once you know he can produce 'ba' you can try to get the sound produced when he sees a 'baby' or a 'ball'. Other easy first words are 'more', 'car' and 'tea'. Think of other words that begin in the same way as one he is beginning to say and see if he can copy them — for example 'bunny', 'bus' and 'book'. This may help the child achieve a sense of success and give him confidence to try more. At first, accept any of his attempts at words, even if they are very faulty. Once he is making a particular sound regularly to denote something, the accuracy of the sound can be licked into shape gradually.

Another way of encouraging sounds is to imitate animal noises or traffic noises. You can play a game of being a cat or a dog, or make the sounds for his toys or for pictures in a book. Cars, aeroplanes and engines, fire engines and police cars all have sounds you can copy and encourage the child to use, as have clocks and bells and telephones.

Imitation

A great deal of learning depends on imitating others. The ability to watch and listen to what someone else does, then trying to do the same is a very important one. Part of the skill also depends on the child being able to observe what he himself is doing, closely enough to know whether his copy is good enough, or whether he can make a better attempt.

With some children the ability to imitate does not seem to come naturally and it may need to be encouraged. If you notice that the child is able to imitate gestures and actions very well, but not sounds, then it would be a good idea to seek some professional advice before going much further, because there may be some specific problems. He may have something wrong with nerves or muscles which makes it difficult for him to produce the sounds he wants without a good deal of special training and help.

Usually the small baby begins the process of imitation by imitating himself. He bangs something or coughs and finds it interesting enough to want to do it again. If the people around him show an interest, all the better. When other people imitate his sounds and actions it makes the process even more interesting. If you copy *his* sounds and make a game of it you are well on the way to his wanting to copy *you*. It will soon be possible to start off an action or sound which he has done before and which you know he can manage and encourage him to copy. Only as a last step will he begin to imitate directly things which are new to him. Constantly demanding that he repeat things which are difficult for him may be quite inappropriate.

Try to build up a repertoire of sounds and actions in which the child can join you. For example, rabbits wriggle noses, fish pop lips and vehicles make various noises. There are many animal sounds, varieties of mock coughs and sneezes and a great many actions with jingles. Quite a bit of prompting may be needed to begin with. If the child seems unable or unwilling to take part in clapping games, take his hands gently and guide him as you sing the rhyme, loosening your hold gradually as he begins to take part. Show him how to play with various toys, if he seems not to get the idea, by taking his hands and doing the actions for him. Then try repeating the same actions with one toy while he holds another similar one, and encourage him to do it too. When the child is really showing an interest in imitation you can introduce games like 'O'Grady says' or 'Follow my leader'. Increase the difficulty of the task by getting him to imitate two, and then a few different things one after another in the right order. Get him to copy simple rhythms with a spoon and a box, a drum, a piano or anything which makes a noise. Make loud and soft notes and slow and fast rhythms.

Introduce the idea of delayed imitation. The child has to watch or listen to what you do and then later, on a signal, he has to do the same. The delay may be only seconds to begin with, longer as he gets better at the game. The point is that eventually you want him to be able to copy, practise and produce sounds which he remembers hearing, when the model is no longer there except in his memory.

The first attempts at sound imitation may be very crude and a long way from being clear and intelligible. You should show pleasure, however, first for any sound at all, and then when the child is producing a meaningful sound consistently for a particular thing. When that sound is being made confidently you can hold out a little longer, for something slightly closer to the word you want, before you show your pleasure and satisfaction. Gradually the word will be 'shaped' correctly.

Language Must be Useful

As the child finds making noises easier and you feel that he is showing an interest in listening and understanding, progress will be made more quickly if he finds that sounds are not just part of a game, fun as that might be, but can be linked with everyday situations and serve a valuable purpose. Using sound to communicate must be rewarding for the child. Get him to use sound in order to have his needs and wishes attended to. Try not to accept his actions and gestures without sounds and do not 'understand' what he is getting at too readily. Often, for the sake of a peaceful life, parents build up a very good understanding with their child, which makes it unnecessary for him to make the effort required to communicate through speech. It is not necesary to discourage the child's gestures but, rather, not to accept them on their own, and to place more emphasis on the sounds in preference to them as the child gets into the habit of making sound.

Make sure that he is given the thing he is asking for *immediately* as a reward, as soon as he makes a good spoken effort to tell you what he wants.

It is important to remember that for the child sound-making should be enjoyable and should bring rewards. Many rhymes and games have their own built-in reward. Making sounds should not be a task or a test for the child and it is important to resist the temptation to get him to show off his growing skills to friends and relatives. That is not usually very pleasurable for him and it makes him fear that he is not going to succeed and will disappoint you. Accept his slow progress in as relaxed and happy a way as you can and you will really be helping him.

Making Sense of Experience

We may need to help a child to develop his understanding of the world. To begin with the small child handles and explores his toys and the things in his immediate world, showing interest in their shape, their feel, their colours and the noises they can make when shaken or banged or thrown. With some very slow children it is necessary to encourage this kind of exploration.

The next step is when the child shows that he is beginning to understand that things 'mean' something. He picks up a cup and instead of just banging it on the table he shows that he understands and remembers what it is used for by pretending to drink from it. He uses a brush to brush his own and then Teddy's hair. He knows that certain things belong to particular people and that some things go together. If a child shows delay in developing any of these ideas you can help him by emphasising the *uses* and *associations* of objects throughout the day, trying to build meaning into things for him. When setting the table you can show him that a knife goes with a fork, a cup with a saucer and while tidying up you can identify things — Daddy's slippers, big sister's coat, and so on.

Using Symbols

Once the very earliest stages have passed, our ability to reason and understand the world is dependent on our ability to use symbols to stand for real things. Communication, and eventually spoken language, is really a process of building up an agreed code of symbols which two people both understand. Words are symbols for things and usually the child's increasing ability to use words is interwoven with his ability to think and use the ideas the words stand for. Before words come, however, children need practice in how to use symbols. Some children with delayed speech are particularly poor in this area and games and activities can help.

Miniatures

Children's toys are often miniatures of real things. Dolls, dolls' houses and furniture, model animals and cars are often very detailed and accurate representations. Until a child has reached a certain stage of development, however, he may not interpret them as such. The child who carries a doll around by the hair or upside down, or the one who uses toy cars to bang with or just to spin the wheels is not really seeing what they 'mean' and his mother may comment, 'Ordinary toys just don't seem to interest him'.

A child may need to be taught to understand what miniatures represent. If possible take the toy and compare it with the real thing, pointing out the similar parts, making the right noises and so on. Start him off with large toys such as dolls and cars and introduce smaller toys gradually. Build in meaning by playing with the toys appropriately showing that *you* understand what they are meant to be. For example, talk to the doll, comfort it, feed it, dress it and sing to it. Put it to bed gently and carefully, making sure that the covers are tucked in properly and are not over the doll's face. In short, try to encourage as much detailed attention and consideration as you would want for a real baby.

Pictures

We often assume that children have the ability to understand pictures without difficulty but this is far from true. Full understanding of how to look at and use pictures may need to be encouraged. Objects can be linked with pictures, getting the child to take the picture of the table to the table and the picture of the orange to the real orange. Later on he can be asked to bring an object or find it from a collection of things when shown a picture. He can be shown a real dog or a toy dog and asked to find a picture of a dog in a book. You can make animal or vehicle noises and ask him to find the picture which fits. At a more advanced stage it is worthwhile studying and talking about more complex pictures with the child, guiding him by the things you pick out into seeing the meaning of the picture, showing him where to start and how to make sense of what is going on.

Memory

Remembering is a very basic part of thinking. At the simplest level a child must learn that, although an object has gone from his view, it is still there somewhere and can be found again. Hiding a teddy bear or other attractive toy behind your back, trying to keep him interested in it, teaching him how to find it, letting it keep peeping out until he goes after it, can start off this kind of thinking. Then this can be extended to all kinds of seeking and finding games. Things which appear and disappear — marble runs, trains going through tunnels, games where pulling a string causes something to happen — all are useful for

encouraging thinking and remembering. You can play the same game, or tell the same simple story over and over again, letting the child guide you as to what comes next once he is familiar with it.

Imagination and Pretend

Imagination comes into many of the things we have been talking about, as for example in putting the doll to bed, or driving a toy car around making 'brrm brrm' noises. Pretend play can be encouraged by playing with dolls, teddy bears or toy rabbits, taking them shopping, doing the housework or having a tea party. You may find you have to teach a child to play in this way at first by making up little scenes and taking him through play situations, suggesting what should happen next. He will enjoy going through the same bit of pretend play many times and eventually he will take over and begin to add new ideas of his own.

Where Are We Up To?

Having got to this point you may feel that this is all too simple and that the child you have in mind is already beyond the stage we have been talking about. Many children, however, will be quite good at some things and very poor at others. It is necessary to look for the gaps which the child may show and try to think of ways to encourage him with the things he finds hard.

Parents may feel that they already do all the things we have been talking about, so before going on to more advanced things, it may be useful to check through the list:

(1) Is the child watching you and listening?
(2) Is he joining in and responding?
(3) Is he enjoying making a variety of sounds?
(4) Is he using sound for a purpose?
(5) Is he imitating?
(6) Is he remembering and searching for things?
(7) Is he able to use small toys appropriately and respond to pictures meaningfully?
(8) Is he showing that he understands what things are and what they are associated with?
(9) Is he beginning to pretend in his play?

If the answer to all these questions is 'Yes', then the child is well on the way to having the right foundations for speech and language, and some of the skills on which to build.

CHAPTER 3

The Development of Higher-level Skills

So far we have been talking about the foundations of language and of the skills which a child needs before he can use words at all, and in the early stages of using them. But once the child is beginning to talk, even a little, then we need to move on.

It is important that a child's attempts at words or phrases should be recognised and welcomed, or 'reinforced'. Similarly, his successes in understanding should be given appreciation and approval. Early on, a child's attempts to talk to you may sound like 'telegram talk', with most of the linking words missed out. This should be accepted as completely normal and not 'corrected'. But the adult should put the little words back in when he replies (so that the child has a correct model) and he will then sort it out for himself in time. Similarly, there is no need to be too concerned about poor pronunciation. But it is worth trying to include his faulty words, correctly pronounced, in what you say back to him. Some children gradually correct their own articulation mistakes as they grow. Others may need help from a speech therapist at some time, but at this stage it is far more important to encourage a child's ability to use language in his thinking and to get him to want to communicate.

Talking to the Child

The way parents talk *to* their child continues to be very important, and as he progresses what is said to him needs to keep pace with his understanding. In the early stages we have talked about ways of simplifying your speech, cutting it into short sentences, emphasising important words and commenting on things that are actually there, or activities you are both engaged in. At times speech can interfere with the child's play and attention and you have to use your judgement about when to talk and when to remain silent.

As time goes on and the child is able to understand more, and is perhaps using a few words himself, he will benefit from more conversation with you. In what *you* say you can help him to plan his play and activities, guiding and suggesting as well as commenting. You may introduce questions, for example, trying to put them into a form which requires a little more than 'yes' or 'no' for an answer. Make it 'Where are you going?' as you see him leaving the room, rather than 'Are you going to the toilet?' Do not get into habit of asking lots of questions which are just for the sake of talking and where both you and the child are aware that you do not really care about the answer. At the same time, avoid turning your conversation into a permanent inquisition.

Give the child the opportunity to make choices and to think things out for himself. Ask him 'Which kind of biscuit would you like today?', or 'Would you rather draw or play with the blocks?'

When he does begin to produce some simple phrases or sentences show great interest in what he says and try to develop it into a conversation. Use ideas which he obviously understands already and try to introduce a little more. (Child) 'Daddy — gone.' (Mother) 'Yes, Daddy's gone to work.' (Child) 'Mo — drink.' (Mother) 'More drink, please? You want some more to drink? Give me your cup then.'

In talking to the child in this way several things are being achieved. You are *expanding* his speech, giving him the opportunity to hear slightly more developed language than that he is using, at a level he is ready for. Your speech contains a lot of *repetition*, with a little variation each time, which helps him to remember and learn, and plenty of *redundancy*. By 'redundancy' is meant language which is not strictly necessary to convey the basic meaning but which is there because it provides useful and varied repetition and extension and so gives the child experience of language.

Think of the way you talk to the child, in response to the very imperfect language he is producing as 'embroidering' *his* speech, just a little, and giving it back to him in the correct form. Do not correct him or try to instruct him *directly*, but gently and unobtrusively give him an immediate example of the correct pronunciation and grammatical form, while showing an interest in what he is saying. In this way you are being constructive and encouraging rather than critical and off-putting. 'Teddy — foots — big', says the child, and you might reply, 'Are Teddy's feet too big? Won't the socks go on?'

Extending Memory and Attention

In order to relate one idea to another and to cope with longer sentences a child's memory and attention must be improving all the time. In the last chapter we talked about encouraging memory in a simple way, by playing with things which appear and disappear. As the child understands more you can do many things to encourage him to take things in and then recall them later.

You can play games where you ask him to listen while you name an object. He must go and touch the object or point to a picture of it in a book. Then name two objects at a time and later three. He must find the objects in the right order. Use familiar story books with pictures and encourage him to add bits of the story himself when reminded by the pictures. Later you can look at pictures or cards together, naming each thing and laying it face down. When there are several laid out you can ask 'Can you find the baby?' 'Which one had a dog on it?' Sets of

'Snap' or 'Picture Lotto' cards are useful for such games and a variety of them is available cheaply at newsagents or toy shops.

Once the child has the idea you can make the game harder in various ways. Lay out the cards face up. Show him a sample card briefly then close your hand over it, asking if he can find another one like it among the cards on the floor. Or, lay out half the cards in another room; give the child one card and ask him to go and find another like it. At first let him take the card but later let him see it only briefly so that he has to remember while searching. As he gets good at this you can ask without showing a picture: 'Bring me the card with a house'; or, more difficult: 'Bring me the house and the chicken and the bell'.

Shuffle the cards and lay them out face down on the carpet. Take turns at choosing two cards. If you find two alike you win the pair, otherwise you turn them face down again. Some children soon become very good at remembering just where particular cards are to be found. Others may need a lot of practice, using only a few cards at a time.

Scatter toys or small objects about the room and give the child a shopping list. This can be a page of drawings to begin with, a verbal list of things to be remembered as he gets better at it. Send him off to collect the items in a basket, then check the list through with him and give him a star in a little book or a small sweet for every one he has got right. Then give him a basket with two objects in it and instructions about what is to be done with each. 'The dolly goes in the cupboard, the pencil in the box.' Later you can extend this by using more objects and making the instructions more complicated. See if he can remember to carry out

the instructions in the right order.

Put a number of objects or pictures on a tray. Have the child close his eyes and take one away, or put a box over it. Open eyes: 'Which one has gone?'

Let the child choose a selection of objects to put into a large cardboard box. Then he can try to remember and tell you what you will find in the box and he gets a swing round or an assisted jump off a chair for each one he remembers correctly. There are countless variations on such games. You can make up your own, increasing the difficulty as the child seems ready for it.

Rehearse things with the child. If for example you are going to go out to buy a stamp and post a letter, go through what is going to happen, step by step, and talk about it together, perhaps making a few drawings or acting it out with dolls or teddy bears. Then when you do go out describe each activity, getting him to suggest what you do next. Back at home, go through it again as a shopping game, getting him to remember and suggest the things you did.

Developing the Ability to Play

Play is essential for a child's healthy development. It is not merely a way in which he keeps himself happily occupied, though it is clearly enjoyable. It is, even more importantly, a way of learning and practising new skills and of developing thinking, language and understanding of others. Through play a child can be creative and he can also learn how to compete and co-operate with others.

Most children play naturally and spontaneously, using whatever they find around them, increasing the detail and complexity of what they are doing as their experience and thinking ability develop. Unfortunately, children who are slow with language often remain stuck at a very simple level of play. Perhaps as babies they were too placid and still, or too active and lacking in concentration. A child can be encouraged best by your joining in his play, getting down on the floor and taking an active part, entering into the spirit of things and trying to make the activities interesting and enjoyable for yourself as well as for him. In the last chapter we talked a good deal about simple play with the child. As he progresses he will become more skilful in handling toys and will perhaps like puzzles of various kinds and construction toys.

Particularly important for the development of language is the kind of play which uses imagination or pretend; this is a gradual development. We have already talked about the way a child begins to show that objects mean something to him by the way he pretends to drink from an empty cup, for example, or by the way he begins to use miniature toys or pictures. These are signs that he is adding something from inside his own head in playing with his toys. Often simple toys encourage imaginative play better than very detailed, complicated ones. It is a good idea to keep a few special toys on one side which you can bring out for a game of 'Let's pretend'. Make the toys *do* things. Dolls or teddy bears can jump or dance, eat and drink, get dressed and go for walks or go to bed. This kind of doll play is equally as important for boys as for girls. Set the scene for the child, with a table and toy cups, or with cars, houses and garages. Let him copy daily household activities by washing the doll's dishes, making his own bit of pastry into a cake, taking the dolls for a walk or mowing the lawn with his push toy. Use all kinds of familiar daily activities to play out stories and situations. Pretend to go shopping, do the housework, have a tea party, go to bed, get up and get dressed or go on journeys or holidays.

Talk about what you are doing, at the level the child seems ready for, at first in short repetitive phrases, leaving gaps for the child to fill. As the child's play becomes fuller and richer you will realise that he is able to understand more and more ideas and your language can become gradually more complicated.

Play pretend-games before and after outings, or in connection with any big experiences, or things which may have worried and puzzled your child, or made him excited. You can play at taking the dolls to the doctor or the dentist. Or, pretend to pack ready to go on holiday, to catch the train and so on. Do not be afraid to go over the same scene again and again. Children often need and want to do this.

Gradually move from big, realistic toys to smaller or less detailed ones. Once your child is really getting the idea of pretending you will find that an old cardboard box can be a bus, a row of blocks becomes a train and the child will be able to pay you in your role as shopkeeper with pretend pennies from an empty purse.

Dressing up is fun in itself and it also helps the child to imagine that he is the postman bringing you a parcel, the doctor listening to your chest or the elegant lady going out shopping. Play through little scenes set in shops, hospitals, restaurants, schools, birthday parties and so on. A Wendy house made of card-board, or a corner screened off with chairs or curtains is good for encouraging this kind of play.

Change over roles sometimes. You be the shopkeeper or the doctor and let him be the Mummy bringing along his teddy. Or you pretend to be the child and let him order you around a little.

Another kind of play which develops gradually is social play, which prepares the child for getting on with other children. Games which encourage the idea of co-operation, taking turns and sharing are all useful preparation for later group activities. You can bring in the other children in the family in various ways. Throwing and catching games, see-sawing, pushing another child on a swing or in a cart and then taking a turn to be pushed, and chasing games of many kinds all are early ways of bringing the child into contact with other children. Later on, simple board games such as picture-lotto or those with simple rules involving waiting turns to throw a dice and move a counter will become possible.

Encouraging the First Words

You will remember from the description of normal speech development that once the child has covered the groundwork for speech he will usually begin to produce his version of the names of familiar people and everyday objects together with a few 'demand' words such as 'More!' and 'Up!'. This is where specific language teaching can begin.

It is a good idea to keep six to ten special toys or household objects in a bag, which can be brought out easily and regularly to play a game of finding and naming them. Do not be too direct and demanding when doing this. Try this approach: 'Here's a ball. What have I got? I've got a . . .' Then show great pleasure as soon as the child responds. Once he really knows the names of the first ten objects then you can get him to tell you the names more directly, and he will be delighted with himself. He must start to feel confident about a few words before he will begin to extend the number of words he uses.

Now you can teach him more and more names for the things you use in the house and that you see outside. Try to find some clear pictures in books and magazines. Most newsagents have racks of inexpensive children's picture books. One or two can be kept hidden away somewhere until you are ready to look at them with the child. Apart from making the books last longer this creates a special time for him, when he gets your full attention and you will find he becomes more interested, looking and listening and co-operating.

Look for opportunities to use the words he now knows naturally throughout the day. Use each label in a variety of ways: 'Whose favourite book is this?' 'Let's put the book on the table.' 'Open the book.' 'Can you find a cat in the book?'

'Put the book away now.' You can use each word in all kinds of different sentences, so that the child begins to understand about it and does not just think of it as the answer to: 'What's this?'

When the child knows and can use the names of several objects you can use these objects in all sorts of bringing, hiding and finding games as we have already described, getting him to use the words as he plays.

Once the child has acquired a handful of naming words, which he can use in the right way and well enough for people to understand him, it is important not to dwell on this accomplishment by naming, and getting the child to name, everything in sight. If you do, he may get stuck for a long time at this 'labelling' stage and may begin to talk in strings of single naming words. Once he has achieved some success in this direction it is time to move on to the next step.

Introducing Action Words

When you think the child knows twenty or so naming words quite well and is using them, begin to include some action words quite deliberately in your teaching. This may mean just a change of emphasis as you talk to him. Instead of stressing the word 'bath' at bath-time you might now emphasise the word 'wash'. 'Wash your hands with the soap.' 'I'll wash your knees.' 'You wash your tummy.' You may say 'Here's your milk', but then think of the action word that goes with it, 'Drink it up. I'll drink mine. You drink yours. Drink the last drop. That's good.' Make sure that you associate the word with the action as you do it.

The same applies to other action words you might use — e.g. come, go, jump, sit, shut, lie down, eat, sleep, carry, and so on.

Children love playing games where they have to do what you do or what you say. Begin by concentrating on three or four action words and play simple games with the child where the actions are repeated over and over again. Dolls and teddy bears can be included in the game. For example, you and the child and all the toys must drink from a cup in turn, or jump, or lie down, the instruction being given each time the action is performed. You can sing action rhymes such as 'This is the way we wash our hands (etc.)', emphasising the action word as the actions are performed each time.

Playing with a ball is one useful way of giving many action words meaning but remember that for this purpose the game must be controlled by language. The adult could be saying, 'Wait. Shall I throw or kick it? Good, you caught it. Now what are you going to do?', encouraging a response before the action and then saying the word again along with the action.

Everyday Phrases and Simple Sentences

The next stage is to encourage the child to put two words together. If he has acquired some naming words and some action words he should be ready for such combinations as, 'baby — sleep', 'kick — ball', 'car — crash', 'drive — bus', and he may also try things like 'nice pussy', 'dinner — gone' and 'bye-bye Daddy'. You can look for opportunities to encourage two words together in all kinds of play and when looking at picture books. Sometimes one word that he knows can be linked with lots of others, 'Bye-bye Daddy, bye-bye doggy, bye-bye car'. Watch out for signs that the child is beginning to put words together himself and in encouraging this try to keep to words that he already knows well. It works best to use reduced repetitive language yourself. You might say while looking at a book, 'Look, the man is driving the bus. You tell me what he is doing — driving the bus.' (Child) 'Drive — bus.' Use the habit of almost talking to yourself as you go over the phrase you are teaching. You can also at this stage encourage two-word phrases about things that belong together, 'John's coat', 'my dinner', 'Nana's house', 'Daddy's car'.

Even if you can't draw very well you can draw John's coat and Nana's house. This often leads to two-word phrases asking for you to repeat an activity, 'more houses', 'draw again'. Another kind of early two-word phrase involves requests along with an idea of appearance/disappearance. Such phrases are often used at meal times, 'all gone', 'another one', 'milk gone', 'more dinner'. Others reflect straight demands, 'want sweet', 'give biscuit'.

Words that are linked up with naming words to point things out around the house or in picture books can be encouraged. 'That's a car.' 'This is an apple.' 'There's a lady.' Holding the child's finger gently and using it to point to the things you want him to notice in a picture book increases his attention and prompts him to try to use 'That's a baby', rather than just 'baby'.

Questions

The child should now be starting to understand the question word 'What?' so when looking at picture books you can ask questions about people, objects and actions. 'What's the boy doing?' (Child) 'Climb — tree.' (Mother) 'Yes, he's climbing the tree. Climbing the tree.' Hopefully when you ask him again he may improve his answer a little. Later you can ask, 'Who's climbing the tree?', trying to encourage a response that will put the three ideas together, 'boy' (subject) — 'climbing' (verb) — 'tree' (object). When you get to this stage you can start asking for commands as to what you are to do in a particular situation: 'Mummy — sit — chair'; 'Daddy — kick — ball'. Most children like to see that they can influence what people do by their words.

Words for Positions

If the child is doing well on all the steps so far it is now time for a new type of game to teach words such as 'in' and 'on' and 'under'. You can start very simply by getting him to put things into a container one by one, say a pile of buttons into a box, saying, '*In* it goes' each time. Then you can sit with the child at a table and

have in front of you a cup and a closed box and a sweet. He has to put the sweet *in* the cup or *on* the box on request. When he gets it right he can have the sweet as a reward (or a hug or just your praise if you prefer). If he gets it wrong you shake your head quietly, ignore it and carry on. Then you can have two cups, one the right way up and one upside down. Can he now manage 'in' and 'on'? You can involve the child himself in action to establish the idea of positions, getting him to sit *in* a box or *on* a chair on request or he can place his teddy in the same way. When he is quite sure of in/on you can teach more difficult position words such as under/on top/behind/beside/in front of, and so on in the same way. You can hide things around the room and give instructions about where they are to be found, 'Look *behind* the big chair; *inside* your toy lorry'. Then you can ask, 'Where did you find it?'

While you are concentrating on position words, think throughout the day how you can emphasise such words as you are going about your ordinary activities.

Opposites

The earliest opposite words to appear are usually big/little. To teach this idea you might take a big spoon and a little one. Teach the child to find the one you ask for by going over it again and again. When you think he has got the idea play the same game with different objects, perhaps a big shoe and a little shoe. Extend the game gradually and at the same time start to point out the difference in size of things you see around the house. Later on you can begin to teach other 'opposite' ideas, such as empty/full, open/shut, long/short, heavy/light, good/naughty, hot/cold, always in situations which are meaningful for the child.

One of a Kind and More Than One

Another idea which the child will be ready for around this stage is that of the singular/plural rule. Usually we add an 's' to the end of a word when we are talking about more than one thing and this is the rule that children understand first, and most easily.

Have a group of similar objects. Take one out and get the child to name it. Then talk about the group of objects using the plural word. Many children are not able to make a very good 's' sound to begin with but they need to appreciate that there is a sound at the end of the word that modifies the meaning. If you exaggerate the sound a little the child will become aware of it and will usually try to add some sound at the end which is good enough at this stage.

Building On

When a child has gone through this range of games, activities and ideas he will be able to talk about a limited number of things, but in many different ways. He will be able to name objects; describe actions; link an object and an action together; state to whom an object belongs; point out objects; state that an object has gone or that an activity has stopped; describe the position of an object; say something about an object in addition to its name, and he will also have begun to put three words together to say who does what to what.

Now he is ready to build on all these aspects. To begin with he can cope with only one idea at a time, then he puts two together. If he is going to be able to extend his language he needs to be able to hold three, four or five ideas at a time and he also needs to learn more of the rules that govern language.

Extending Sentence Complexity

The way in which children use sentences usually goes through stages of increasing complexity. For example:

Stage 1. Daddy. Gone.

Stage 2. Kick — ball. That — car. Big — doll. In — car.

Stage 3. Daddy — gone — work. Ball — in — box. That — baby — naughty. Bird — fly — away.

Stage 4. Baby — eat — my — cake. Me — play — ball — garden.

As you can see the number of ideas linked together is increasing. You can help this process along in various ways.

Help the child to string little sentences together, first by using 'and'. For example, while looking at pictures together you can say, 'The little boy is going shopping *and* then he's going to the park *and* then he's coming home for tea.' Talking about pictures together, working out the stories behind the pictures can be of great help at this stage. Then using simple story books, such as those of the Ladybird series, which have good clear action pictures, you can ask the child 'why', 'who' and 'how' questions and help him to construct sentences beginning with 'because'. This helps him to see how one action follows another and how one idea relates to the next. For example: 'Why is the dog swimming in the pond?' (Child) 'Because he's going to fetch the ball.' 'Why is the ball in the water?' (Child) 'Because the little boy kicked it in.' 'How is the dog going to bring it back?' (Child) 'In his mouth.'

Extending Grammar

A child usually picks up grammatical rules as he is ready for them, often going through a stage where he makes odd-sounding mistakes for a while as he tries out a new rule. The little boy who says, 'I *eated* up my dinner', has obviously learned that '*ed*' added to the end of a word usually means that the action was in the past. Unfortunately the English language has many such irregular verbs. If you find an oppertunity to say the correct word when replying to the child, 'Yes, that's a good boy, you ate all your dinner', rather than correcting him, he will sort it out in time.

In general you can teach the regular and most common rules by little games. For example, to teach verb tenses you might have the child stand on a chair and then say, 'What are you going to do — are you going to jump?' Hold his hands and say 'You're jumping', as he does the action, and then afterwards, 'You jumped. What did you do? You jumped.' It is useful to think about ways of putting meaning into whatever you want to teach by involving the child in action and demonstration as you use the words.

Associations

The ability to see relationships, similarities and connections betwen things is a very important one and is the basis of a great deal of human thought, language and higher-level learning. This ability normally develops alongside language so that talking and thinking grow together.

Objects vary in many different ways and the child needs to be able to group together things which are similar in some way, so that he can think about the idea which connects them. For example he may put together all the things that are red from among his toys or all the things that are round.

Matching

The first stage is to encourage the child to match things exactly by, for example, finding another block which is just like the one you are holding, in shape and size and colour. Or he can be set to find an identical picture. Early on you can get him inset boards, where he has to find the right shape for the inset, or simple jigsaw puzzles and shape-posting boxes of various kinds. Games like Picture-Bingo, colour and picture dominoes and 'Snap' all involve matching. Start with simple straightforward matching. Then you can move on to finding something which might not be exactly the same in all respects. For example he might have to find 'another car' of a different make. The easiest matching ideas are those of colour and size. Then come shape and texture, followed by more complicated or more abstract categories.

You can go on to matching by association, 'Here is a picture of a nail. Which of these other things do we use to bang it in?' Or, 'This one is a mummy cow. Which of these baby animals belong to her?' Connections such as where animals live, what they eat, what sounds they make, what people wear, which things are used together, can be used in order to decide how to put pictures or objects together.

Sets of cards or picture books are useful for these 'linking things together' games and it is also a good idea to cut out clear attractive pictures from old magazines or catalogues, keeping them in a box for this purpose, adding to the collection all the time, and throwing away pictures as they become tattered.

Sorting

Try to get the child interested in sorting things into groups. All the toy cars go in one box, all the dolls and teddy bears in another, all the books on the shelf. To begin with start him on sorting out things which are *very* different. Make up a bag of plastic animals and marbles, to be sorted into two transparent boxes, so that he can see what he has already put in. Expect mistakes to begin with and keep on showing him gently what you want until he gets the idea.

Next you might take a bag of mixed blocks and start building a tower, using only the yellow blocks, asking the child to find more blocks for you. When he gets the idea, start again and build a blue tower. Give the child the name for the colour you are using but do not expect him to be able to find 'a red one' when you ask for it, or to tell you that a particular toy is 'red' until he has had a great deal of practice.

Once the child is able to do this sort of thing you can make up all kinds of groupings, talking about why the things go together and giving the collection word for the group as you go. 'Yellow things', 'round ones', 'marbles', 'animals'. Move on gradually to more complicated groupings. For example, put all the pictures of things to eat in one pile, or stick them on one page of a scrap book, all the pictures of furniture on another. Sort things in one way and then mix them up and sort in a different way — 'This time instead of looking for chairs let's find all the pictures which have children on them.'

Sort out the bag of blocks into different colours, then into different shapes with the colours mixed. Then make it harder by looking for two things at once: 'See if you can find all the blocks which are red *and* round.'

Now you can introduce games of 'Find the odd one out'. This is a difficult idea, even for children who are quite good at sorting and matching, so go slowly. Start with simple ideas again. You might put three similar round blocks together, two blue and one red and ask, 'Which one is different?' Or take a handful of marbles with one large button among them and see if your child can find the one that 'shouldn't be there' or 'isn't like the others'. Talk about why the odd one is different.

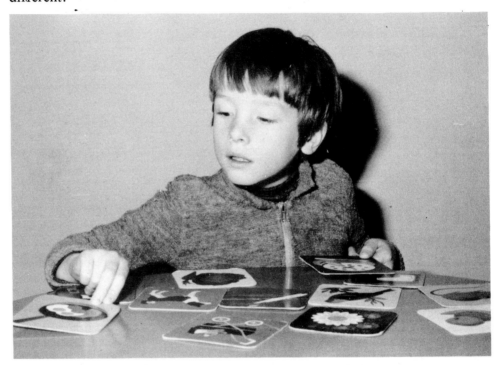

You may have to use all sorts of ways of explaining this idea before it finally clicks. As the child begins to understand what he is looking for you can increase the difficulty until for example you have several different 'things for sitting on', with a table as the odd one out, or several farm animals with a lion among them. All of these games, in addition to teaching ideas, form a useful setting for a lot of conversation and experience of words.

Grading or Ordering

Another important thinking activity involves putting things in order. We grade

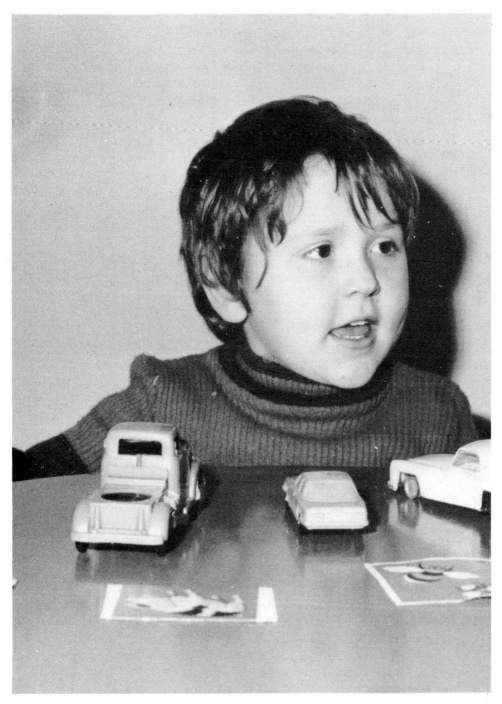

things according to many different dimensions: long/short, big/small, many/few, empty/full, heavy/light, rough/smooth, and so on. Many inset puzzles encourage the ability to grade by making it necessary for the child to find, for example the smallest cat, then the next biggest and so on. Nesting boxes or

dolls which pack away inside each other need the same kind of ability, as do various stacking toys. Talk about the ideas while helping the child with such toys, or showing an interest in what he is doing — 'First the little baby one, then the bigger one, then the biggest one of all.'

You can build useful practice in matching, sorting and grading into many of the games you play with the child. Lay out objects or pictures around the room, show him a sample picture and ask him to find one like it, or at a higher level something that goes with it in a particular way, like a knife with a fork or a cup with a saucer. You can play 'I spy' and ask the child to find, 'Something that is round and red'. Use a big cardboard box for a post-box, on which you can hold the flap closed, only opening it to admit things with some quality you have asked for, 'Any picture with an animal on it' or 'Things that are good to eat'. You can make picture scrap-books, sticking things which are alike in some way on the same page and then making up a story about them. Once you have started thinking in this way the opportunities for teaching a child through play and everyday activities are endless.

Faults of Early Speech

Language usually develops rapidly between the ages of eighteen months and four years and during that time the child's *articulation* improves and his 'sound system' expands. This begins in a limited way and becomes increasingly clearer, with a wider range of sounds being used as language develops. It is quite normal for a child to be substituting some of the easier sounds for some of the harder ones until he is about six or seven years old. For example, many children substitute an 'f' or a 'v' for 'th' ('fevver' for 'feather') or a 'w' for an 'r' ('wed for 'red', or 'wight' for 'right') until long after they have started school.

As the child learns to listen to sounds made by others in speech and to notice his own versions he is likely to vary his 'errors' in his attempts to correct himself before he finally reaches the adult version. You may notice that for a period he can use a particular sound correctly in some words or positions and not in others. For example 'dog' may be pronounced 'gog' although 'daddy' is said correctly. This is not just cussedness or laziness on the child's part; the process is just a lot more complex than we usually allow for.

The great majority of pronunciation mistakes will come right by themselves as the child matures. However, there are some children who may have a bigger problem, and who find such difficulty in making certain sounds that they are unlikely to get over this without some expert speech therapy help. If parents are worried because their child remains difficult to understand for a long period, they should not hesitate to ask the advice of the local Speech Therapy Service.

Some children go through a phase when they seem to be speaking quite well, but are repeating a great deal of what they hear around them and are not really telling you anything. In extreme cases their speech may be made up entirely of parts of what you have just said to them. This is because they have learned to copy and to remember what they hear but they have not yet attached real meaning to the words. In fact *echolalia*, as it is called, is usually a sign that a child is not fully understanding what he is hearing.

If this happens it is essential to go back and put the emphasis on the *meaning* of words in everyday situations, using plenty of simple reduced language as we have suggested earlier. If parents go through the earlier stages of building up understanding, looking at books with a child and using everyday situations, then the echolalia will gradually disappear.

Helping Clearer Speech

Parents often want to know how they can help their child to speak more clearly and there are a few simple rules which can help, once the basic groundwork for language is established.

(1) Make a point of speaking clearly but naturally yourself. Repeat sounds which the child is omitting or using incorrectly in what you say back to him, exaggerating them just a little. Do not get into the habit of correcting him every time.

(2) Do not split the initial sound in a word from the rest of it. For example, when trying to get the child to say a word there is a temptation to try to get

him going by emphasising the initial sound — 'p–ie' for 'pie'. It is better to try to get the sounds used together, by babbling or repeating the example — 'pie pie pie'.

(3)   If the child is omitting final sounds slow down the word as you say it to him, slightly exaggerating the final sound — 'po-*p*', 'bu-*s*'. Be careful not to put an extra sound on the end, however, making it 'po-peh' and 'bu-seh'.

(4)   Try to focus on words containing 'p', 'b', 'm', 't' and 'd' and get those clear first of all. Then try words with 'k', 'c' and 'g'. For example start with words like 'ball', 'book', 'tea', 'door', 'pie' and 'more', before going on to words like 'car', 'girl', 'gun' and 'kick'.

(5)   Play games with sounds: 'k-k-k-k' for the noise of guns, 's-s-s-s' for snakes, 'sh-sh-sh-sh' for quiet games.

(6)   Try to get an 's' at the ends of words when appropriate, by exaggerating the sound a little as you make it, even if the child is not yet able to make an 's' at the beginning of a word.

(7)   If he is slow in getting sounds sorted out do not expect him to be able to use blends of sounds, where there are two or more consonants together — e.g. *pl*ay, *br*ing, *st*op. He needs to master the simpler sounds first.

(8)   Make a little time each day when you give the child all your attention and talk to him or read him a short story while he is listening, in a quiet, calm atmosphere.

Stammering

Between the ages of three-and-a-half and five years a considerable number of children go through a phase when they find it difficult to speak smoothly and fluently. They have many ideas that they are eager to talk about. They are beginning to think in a more complicated way about the things that happen around them and their interaction with other people. They have feelings and thoughts to express, but the use of words, the rules of grammar and the order of words which they use to talk are still being mastered. Words or parts of words sometimes become stammered or repeated, almost as if the child is filling in and playing for time while he organises what he wants to say. Sometimes children rush at words in a state of great excitement and the carefully controlled movements required to pronounce a complicated sentence cannot be managed. The child repeats and sometimes even 'blocks' completely in his search for ordered speech. This is a stage which will normally pass as the child develops more experience in talking. Over-reaction, by annoyance or scolding, impatience and turning away or obvious anxiety can make the child even more uncertain of his speech. Even telling him frequently to stop and start again can have this effect and the complicating feelings of guilt or anger or worry in the child can lead to his becoming a long-term stammerer.

The best approach is to accept the hesitations and stammering with little obvious reaction. This can be difficult, particularly if the parent, or a relative, has had a similar problem. For this reason it might be a good idea to refer the child to a speech therapist so that there can be a full discussion about it. It is unlikely that it would be thought necessary for the child to attend a clinic on a regular basis at this stage.

Language and Self-direction

Language is a part of thinking and much of our thinking involves a kind of talking to ourselves, usually silently, inside our heads. We may try to remember directions about how to get somewhere; we plan what we are going to do during the day; we remind ourselves about things, and we talk to ourselves in order to choose one thing rather than another.

A child also needs to learn how to tell himself what to do. This is another ability which usually develops gradually, and we can encourage its development in various ways.

At a very early stage language helps the child to notice, attend and understand only when it is simple, direct and concerned with what he is seeing or doing at the moment. If there is too much talking or instruction he cuts out and is distracted. Once he has developed a little further, however, some adult talking, instructing and suggesting, helps the child to sort things out and think about them. You can get a child used to following instructions from the early months, asking him to give you things, bring you things or point to things, giving him your attention in a pleasurable way so that he wants to co-operate. Gradually you can make your instruction games more complicated, increasing the complexity of your language, getting him to use more than one idea at a time or giving him several instructions to be carried out in order, in the way we have already discussed.

Self-direction

As you set the child tasks such as sorting out all the toys into their different boxes or shelves, setting the table, doing the dusting or putting a series of pictures in order to tell a story, you can break it down and give him the instructions in the form of a recipe. 'First you do this — and then this — and next this.' Rehearse the task with him, getting him to remember the instructions by saying them out loud. Then go through the task with him and see if he can talk himself through it, reminding himself of what to do at each stage.

As you see the child trying to do something quite complicated in his play, encourage him to tell himself what he is doing. To begin with, *you* do the simple running commentary and try to get him to join you by leaving gaps or asking what he is going to do next.

Draw a few pictures to illustrate a favourite story and then ask him to tell the story from the pictures, putting them in order as he goes. With any game where he has to puzzle something out try to get him to put it into words. 'If I pull this string, what will happen? I think the little man will pop up there. Let's see if he does.' 'Now how do I put this back together again? This piece goes here because the red bits go together . . .'

Only when the child has had lots of practice at this sort of thing will he be able to take the words, the explanations and instructions, inside his head in the form of silent 'thinking'. Once he can do this then he will be on the way to independence, able to sort out his experiences and make use of them. He will be able to deal with his moods and frustrations more effectively and he is likely to show fewer behaviour difficulties. All in all he will be a much pleasanter child to have around.

Specifying activities to encourage language development can make the process seem more studied and self-conscious than it is or need be. Most parents are probably already doing a great many of the things we have talked about, perhaps without realising their full significance. So many things can be done in the course of a normal family day, without imposing extra burdens of time and effort, or depriving other members of the family of attention. What is needed with the language-retarded child is a little more organisation and deliberateness in using normal, natural situations and occasions — a slightly tidier version of everyday interactions.

CHAPTER 4

Getting Extra Help

Most of this book has been concerned with how parents can be helped to help their own language-retarded child. All of those involved professionally in the educational and therapeutic services have come to recognise the importance of encouraging such self-help. Professional resources are limited and specialist expertise is not always necessary. There may be a tendency for parents to worry 'unnecessarily' — their concern is, after all, a special one — but they are usually the first to suspect that something may be really wrong with their child's development. In this case it is important that they should not be put off by being told that they are just over-anxious and fussy, and should wait until the child is five-or perhaps seven-years-old, by which time he will have 'grown out of it'. They can be referred to a speech therapist or educational psychologist by their health visitor or general practitioner or, alternatively, they can make the contacts directly. If, after the child has been seen and assessed, they learn that he is progressing quite well and there is no cause for worry, then nothing has been lost. If parents are worried it is far better for the professionals to be able to reassure them than to risk missing the opportunity of helping a child early on when he really needs it.

When is There Cause to Worry about a Child's Speech and Language?

There is great variation in normal patterns of development and no parents should think that their child has serious problems just because he is not talking in the same way as another child they know. However, if certain normal responses are lacking then perhaps some further investigation might help.

Significant Signs between 18 Months and 2 Years

Possible hearing difficulties may be suspected if the child shows little response to noise-making toys, such as rattles or bells. The child with a hearing problem may not always respond to his name or to approaches in words. He may not be startled by sudden noises, unless they are accompanied by vibration, or unless he happens to be looking in the direction of the noise. He may not respond when someone enters the room if he is turned away from the door. He may make many odd sounds himself, with snorts and grunts which do not sound like speech noises.

The hearing of some children fluctuates with colds and ear, nose, throat or other infections. Other children may be hearing some types of sounds and not others. It is easy to be deceived: because children learn to pick up so many cues from facial expression, gestures and what is going on around them, they can *appear* to be understanding the words. If parents have doubts about this they should try to cut out all the other clues and see if the child still understands, and if after this they are still uneasy they should ask their health visitor, or family or clinic doctor about possible tests.

There is cause for concern if a child is *very unresponsive* — if he is silent and seems to have little interest in sounds or if he shows no reaction to games like 'Pat-a-cake' or 'Peek-a-boo' and does not join in. He may show no interest in the names of everyday objects, or in fetching and carrying games. He may not seem to want to move about and explore things, or to examine and play with toys. He may show little ability to occupy himself in play and may be making no attempt to use sounds or little words. It is particularly important to note whether he copies gestures and expressions easily but not sounds.

Of particular concern is the child who seems *completely out of contact*, avoiding listening to and looking at people, living in a world of his own. He may have many little mannerisms and obsessions and he may have frequent and ferocious temper tantrums.

A child who has a lot of *difficulty with chewing and swallowing* may also have problems with speech. It is important to distinguish however between the child who is having real difficulty and the one who is playing up at meal times for attention.

Significant Signs between 3 and 4 Years

With some children problems may not have been very noticeable in the early years but have become apparent a little later on as they fail to develop normally. Some of the following signs may appear.

(1)   The child may be 'fluent' in that he talks a lot and seems to have plenty that he wants to say, but he is intelligible only to those who know him well, and not always to them.
(2)   The child may be making a lot of vowel and nasal sounds or using a limited range of sounds with many needed sounds missing from his speech.
(3)   The child may not appear to understand what is said to him, except for the very simplest things.
(4)   The child may be able to speak, though not very well, to a few people, but will not attempt to talk to others at all.
(5)   The child may seem to be stuck. He can use a few single words but is

making no attempt to put words together.

(6)   The child may have developed a persistent stammer.

If parents have worries about a child on any of these grounds, or for other reasons not mentioned here, there are a number of things they can do about it.

Local Services and the Kind of Professionals Who Man Them

An early step should be to find out what the local system has to offer. There will be a need for recognition and assessment of the child's problems, for appropriate therapy and other support, and perhaps for decisions about education. Probably the best person to help the parents find their way among the various provisions is the *health visitor*. In some areas there may also be particular health visitors for children with a variety of special needs.

A health visitor is a trained nurse who has specialised in social and community needs. She is often based at a Child Health Centre or at a doctors' surgery and almost all health visitors are attached to a particular doctor's practice. She has links not only with doctors and hospitals but also with community services of various kinds. She knows about local facilities such as playgroups and nurseries and, where appropriate, can arrange to provide equipment for medical or nursing care and give advice on allowances which may be available. She can refer on to medical or other services if necessary and can be a useful ally in making and keeping appointments. Many people think of the health visitor as someone concerned only with babies, who visits during the early months of a child's life and who can also be seen at the Child Health Clinic. In fact she is interested in the child's development at all ages and her help can be sought at any stage.

Screening Assessments and Routine Developmental Checks

Conditions vary in different parts of the country but most Area Health Authorities have some system by which children with special needs, including those with speech delay, can be recognised and provided for at an early stage.

In all areas parents are encouraged to attend local *Child Health Clinics* for routine checks on their child's development in the early years. In addition, in some areas, babies are given screening tests at intervals, usually once between seven and nine months and again at three and a half years. A health visitor normally carries out these checks and looks at such things as vision and hearing, the growth and control of body movements, the co-ordination of sight with fine movements, the development of speech and the understanding of language, social relationships with adults and other children and developing independence in feeding, washing, dressing and so on. If she is concerned about a child's development after one of these screenings the health visitor will probably ask either the family doctor or the clinical medical officer at the Child Health Clinic to have a look at him.

It is likely that a child's problems will be recognised and investigated at some stage, but parents can also take the initiative in talking about their worries and asking for advice. There are many services available but in the last analysis it may well be up to the parents to ensure that their child gets the attention and help he needs at the first opportunity.

The Family Doctor or General Practitioner

If there is concern about a child the family doctor may arrange to see him and may refer him on for further examinations and opinions to various hospital consultants such as paediatricians, ear, nose and throat specialists, audiologists or orthopaedic surgeons, depending on the child's problems.

Most areas now have a *Paediatric Assessment Centre* where a child can be assessed by a variety of professionals in order to give a full picture and the GP or clinic doctor may suggest a referral there. This will involve a lengthy visit to the Centre, of at least a full day and maybe several days, during which time parents and child may see a paediatrician, a psychologist, a physiotherapist, an occupational therapist, a speech therapist, a social worker and possibly several other professionals. If parents are worried about their child's development then they can ask their GP if he could go to the Paediatric Assessment Centre, but of course this may not be appropriate if he is already being seen by a particular consultant.

Clinical Medical Officers

These are the community doctors who are concerned with child development, first in the Child Health Clinics and later in the schools. Like health visitors they have links with both medical and community services. If the clinical medical officer is asked to examine a young child he or she may do so at the clinic or may arrange to see the child and his parents at home. Later on he may be seen again for school medical examinations, which parents are invited to attend.

Social Services

Social workers do not just deal with 'problem families'. They can be very helpful in all sorts of circumstances. Where appropriate they can advise on aids and allowances and can help with adaptations of the home where this is needed for a child. They can offer support when a family is under stress for any reason and can sometimes help out during crises. If a child spends a period in hospital or at a

Paediatric Assessment Centre there may be a social worker who will offer some continuing support for a little while. If parents want to ask for help from Social Services it is usually best for them to contact their office directly to explain the problems. The telephone number is normally listed under '____shire County Council — Social Services Department — Area Offices', and contact is made with the appropriate area office.

The Speech Therapy Service

This is a side branch of the health service and parents can ask to be referred through the health visitor or family doctor or can make contact directly. The telephone number is usually listed under '____shire Area Health Authority — Speech Therapy Clinics'. Contact is first made with the central clinic.

A speech therapist is trained to assess children in order to determine (a) how well the child is understanding, (b) how he is beginning to build up language and (c) how his sound system — his ability to use all the sounds of language — is developing. In most Authorities there are clinics held in various places throughout the area, where children are seen, either individually or in groups. In addition speech therapists often visit special schools of various kinds and Speech Units in ordinary schools on a regular basis. They work in conjunction with parents and other professionals and part of their role is to give guidance to others on how they can best help the child. Particularly with a pre-school child the speech therapist would want to involve the parents as much as possible. She will not be able to 'teach the child to talk' directly unless the problem is merely one of poor pronunciation, which it rarely is. Her 'treatment' will often be concerned with more general activities, trying to get the child using and understanding language, in cooperation with his parents and, where appropriate, his teachers.

The Schools' Psychological Service and Child and Family Guidance Service

In some areas these will be two separate services and in others a combined service. Parents can ask to be referred by various professionals or they can make a direct approach. The telephone number will usually be found under '____shire County Council — Education Department — Schools' Psychological Service and Child Guidance (or Child Guidance and SPS)'.

In spite of the reference to schools in the title, this service has an interest in preschool children who are having any kind of difficulty, or who are presenting handling problems. There are three types of professional within the service — educational psychologists, social workers and psychiatrists. Parents might start off seeing one person and then others might be called on to help. If there are severe problems about a child's development, his behaviour or management then the service provides access to discussion, opinions and advice plus the possibility of various kinds of practical help.

The educational psychologist is the one particularly concerned when there is any question about the need for special educational provision. On the basis of discussions with parents and other people who know the child, and following various tests and observations he will be able to decide on what is most appropriate. He knows the local school system and what may be available for a child with special needs and after discussing this with parents he will make his recommendations to the Local Education Authority. Visits to any special schools or units recommended can always be arranged.

Parents, therefore, have access to several services, either directly or through their health visitor or doctor. If their child is already in school they can also ask for help through the headteacher, the school nurse or the clinical medical officer.

Voluntary Organisations

More general information and guidance can be obtained from pamphlets and reading lists supplied by various voluntary organisations. There are many such organisations concerned with different types of problems and a good source of reference and addresses can be found in two useful booklets:

(1)   'Help starts here' — for parents of children with special needs. Produced by and available from The Voluntary Council for Handicapped Children, National Children's Bureau. 8 Wakley Street, London EC1V 7QE.
(2)   'Handbook for parents with a handicapped child' — by Judith Stone and Felicity Taylor. Available from CASE Publications, 17 Jackson's Lane, Billericay, Essex.

Probably the most important national organisations in Britain to be aware of are the following:

(1)   AFASIC (Association for all Speech Impaired Children).
(2)   ICAA (Invalid Children's Aid Association). This association has a special interest in the problems of speech-impaired children. 126 Buckingham Palace Road, London SW1W 9SB.
(3)   National Society for Mentally Handicapped Children. 117-123 Golden Lane, London EC1Y ORF.
(4)   National Society for Autistic Children. 1A, Golders Green Rd, London NW11 8EA.

The first two associations are relevant for all children with speech and language problems, the latter two only for particular groups of speech-impaired children.

The head office of these and other organisations can give details of local branches and the services they offer. If there is difficulty in finding local addresses it is possible to consult the local library, Citizen's Advice Bureau or the Community Health Council. Addresses of particular national organisations, or answers to questions about individual problems or about services can be obtained by writing to the Voluntary Council for Handicapped Children, National Children's Bureau, 8 Wakley Street, London EC1V 7QE (Tel: 01-278-9441) who will try to help, or advise where help can be obtained locally.

Education

At the Pre-school Level

Local education authorities have the power to provide nursery education within the state system from the age of three years and to provide pre-school education for children with special needs from the age of two years. The extent to which they have done this varies widely and in a particular area there may be a great many facilities or none at all. Health visitors or the Schools' Psychological Service can give advice about local provision.

Again, in a particular area there may be a range of social services, voluntary or private facilities, some of which may involve fees. In general, some of the following may be found:

Local Education Authority. Nursery classes in ordinary schools (often part-time attendance from three to five years). Nursery classes attached to special schools (e.g. schools for the severely subnormal — may be part-time from two years). Special nurseries for handicapped children (often part-time from two years). Peripatetic visiting home teachers for handicapped children, who can visit, often at intervals of a few weeks, from the time the child is discovered to have special needs.

Social Services. Day nurseries — provide a full day's care, including school holidays, usually for families experiencing difficulties. A charge is made on the basis of income.

Voluntary and Private. Special nurseries run by organisations such as the Red Cross or Menphys — sometimes five days a week, more usually on one or two days weekly. Some are for children with different types of problems, e.g. physical/mental handicaps.

Toy Libraries. Non-profit-making centres for lending appropriate toys to handicapped children. Local groups sometimes run parents' associations and act as a useful meeting centre. There are now more than twenty Toy Library Associations throughout the country and there may be one locally. Contact The

Toy Libraries Association, 21 Gentleman's Row, Enfield, Middlesex (Tel: 01-363-1394) for information.

Voluntary Home-teaching Organisations, such as Home-Start. These are usually staffed by parents who have been given a short training and who will go into homes where there is some kind of difficulty in providing for the needs of a child, to help the mother and give suggestions about playing with and stimulating the child. Health visitors or social workers will know of local groups.

Playgroups. There are a great many of these and they normally operate for two or three days a week, but the child can attend for less if desired. The Pre-School Playgroups Association, Alford House, Aveline Street, London SE11 5DJ (Tel: 01-582-8871) can give further information. Health visitors will usually know about local playgroups and the fees they charge.

Other groups. Playgroups of various kinds may be run in connection with hospitals, paediatric assessment centres or speech therapy departments. A child with special needs may be recommended to attend one of these normally once a week by one of the various services mentioned above.

The School System

Most parents hope that their child will manage in an ordinary class in an ordinary school, and many children who early on show speech and language difficulties *will* do so, sometimes with help from weekly speech therapy sessions. Some, however, will not be able to cope and various alternatives may have to be considered when the child reaches school age.

All children are entitled to education from the age of five years. Local Education Authorities are required to make special provision for children with special needs, but this has been interpreted in different ways by different authorities and so there is great variation in what is available in different areas in the way of special schools, special classes or units, or extra help within ordinary schools. There is also variation in the extent to which different authorities use boarding schools for children with special educational needs.

Within the ordinary schools there is usually some provision for a child with learning problems to get extra help, often on the basis of a withdrawal group at certain times in the week. A child with speech and language problems may, in addition, be able to attend a weekly speech therapy session at the local clinic.

All LEAs have special schools for children who are described as slow-learning with severe problems, and most have schools for slow-learning children where the problems are mild. There may also be schools for the physically handicapped, again usually divided into mild and severe problems. There may be schools for maladjusted children, showing behavioural or emotional problems, and schools for the visually handicapped or hearing-impaired. In all these types of schools some children who also show speech and language problems can be accommodated.

Some authorities have developed units attached to ordinary schools for all these types of handicap, sometimes instead of special schools and sometimes in addition to them. Children with speech problems, learning problems or mild hearing problems can often be catered for very well in such units.

Most authorities provide education on a day basis for the majority of their children with special needs, only financing boarding education at a school outside the authority for those children with particularly severe disorders whose needs cannot be met locally. Obviously, if it looks as if a child is going to have special educational needs it is necessary for parents to discuss this with someone who knows the local provision. The most appropriate person is the educational psychologist at the Schools' Psychological Service.

The Rights and Powers of Parents

We list here some of the rights and powers relevant to the parents of a speech-impaired child. Most of them have the greatest relevance in pre-school days and early school-days. Further information about the longer term is given in the two reference booklets mentioned previously.

(1)   Parents have the right to ask for advice. Whenever they see any professional concerning their child they can ask for information and explanations. It may help them to write down any questions they want to ask before the interview.

(2)   They have the right to ask what they can do to help and to ask for *practical* advice from the professionals they see.

(3)   They have the right to ask for help from *various* agencies, either by approaching them directly or by asking someone like a health visitor to do it for them.

(4)   They have the right to ask for various tests, such as vision and hearing tests to be done.

(5)   They have the right to ask their Local Education Authority, usually through its educational psychologists, to examine their child if it is thought he may need special educational provision. (The Authority can also insist on an examination if there is some concern over the child's development.)

(6)   They have a right to full-time education for their child from the age of five. In some cases various types of provision may be available from the age of two or three years.

(7)   They have the right to be told the nature and extent of their child's

disability and to be consulted over any decisions made about him, either medical or educational. And they can challenge these decisions, if they disagree.

(8)   They have the right to join various organisations which offer information and support by enabling them to meet other parents who have faced similar problems.

(9)   They have a right, often through such groups as mentioned in (8) above to exert pressure at a national or local level for reforms and provisions which they think need to be made. Many advances in provision for the handicapped have come through the work of such pressure groups.

Finally, in spite of these rights and powers, and even following the most thorough assessments it may be quite impossible for anyone to tell parents *why* their child shows the difficulties he does. In any case explanations are not usually much help in determining what to do about a child's problems. Whether or not exact causes are known, attempts have to be made to help the child overcome his handicap. The practical problem is that of remediation. The present book is intended as a contribution in this area.

Recommended Further Reading

Practical

Browning, E. (1972) *I Can't See What You're Saying* (London; Paul Elek)

Cook, V.J. (1979) *Young Children and Language* (London: Edward Arnold)

de Villiers, P. and de Villers, J. (1979) *Early Language — Dada* (London: Fontana Books)

Gillham, B. (1979) *The First Words Language Programme* (London: George Allen and Unwin)

Gulliford, R. (1971) *Special Educational Needs*, Chapter 6 (London: Routledge and Kegan Paul)

Jeffree, D.M. and McConkey, R. (1976) *Let Me Speak* (London: Souvenir Press)

Jeffree, D.M., McConkey, R. and Hewson, S. (1977) *Let Me Play* (London: Souvenir Press)

Theoretical

Cooper, J., Moodley, M. and Reynell, J. (1978) *Helping Language Development* (London: Edward Arnold)

Crystal, D. (1976) *Child Language Learning and Linguistics* (London: Edward Arnold)

Francis-Williams, J. (1970) *Children with Special Learning Difficulties* (Oxford: Pergamon Press)

Hersov, L.A., Berger, M. and Nicol, A.R. (1980) *Language and Language Disorders in Childhood* (Oxford: Pergamon Press)

Irwin, J.V. and Marge, M. (1972) *Principles of Childhood Language Disabilities* (New York: Appleton-Century-Crofts)

Morley, M.E. (1965) *The Development and Disorders of Speech in Childhood* (Edinburgh: Livingstone)

Renfrew, C. and Murphy, K. (1964) *The Child Who Does Not Talk* (London: Heinemann Medical Books)

Rutter, M. and Martin, J.A. (eds.) (1972) *The Child with Delayed Speech* (London: Heinemann Medical Books)

About the Authors

Phyllis Hastings is a Senior Speech Therapist in Leicestershire, working mainly in three fields: treatment of voice disorders, group treatment with stroke patients, and the diagnosis, assessment and treatment of young children within a long-term diagnostic and assessment unit.

She trained in Glasgow and worked for three years in a Child Guidance Service. Later, in London, she worked in community clinics and special schools.

She is married with three grown-up children.

Bessie Hayes is a Senior Educational Psychologist in Leicestershire and has a special interest in young handicapped children and problems of language acquisition.

She is a member of the team at a Paediatric Assessment Centre and is concerned with a Speech Class attached to a primary school, in addition to working with Phyllis Hastings in a long-term diagnostic and assessment unit.

After teaching for five years she worked on various research projects in England and America before moving into educational psychology twelve years ago. She has a Master's Degree in Child Psychology from Nottingham University.

She is married with three teenage children.

Index